Nginx Troubleshooting

Investigate and solve problems with Nginx-powered websites using a deep understanding of the underlying principles

Alex Kapranoff

BIRMINGHAM - MUMBAI

Nginx Troubleshooting

First published: April 2016

Production reference: 1190416

Published by Packt Publishing Ltd.
Livery Place
35 Livery Street
Birmingham B3 2PB, UK.

ISBN 978-1-78528-865-4

www.packtpub.com

Credits

Author
Alex Kapranoff

Reviewers
Titouan Galopin
Valery Kholodkov

Commissioning Editor
Dipika Gaonkar

Acquisition Editor
Reshma Raman

Content Development Editor
Sanjeet Rao

Technical Editor
Mohit Hassija

Copy Editor
Dipti Mankame

Project Coordinator
Judie Jose

Proofreader
Safis Editing

Indexer
Priya Sane

Graphics
Kirk D'Penha

Production Coordinator
Shantanu N. Zagade

Cover Work
Shantanu N. Zagade

About the Author

Alex Kapranoff is an established IT professional with more than 20 years of experience in roles ranging from a database developer to the CTO of a social search engine start-up to an infrastructure manager of a huge web application with hundreds of millions of users. His background allows him to be more on the developer side of things, and he is happy to share some of that perspective with fellow system administration specialists.

About the Reviewers

Titouan Galopin is a certified PHP/Symfony French web architect from Paris. He currently works for SensioLabs, the company behind the PHP framework Symfony, and he has worked for various other companies, including LIIP, Emakina, Ademis, and Coburo.

Titouan graduated in computer science and information technology from the Paris-Saclay University, and he is currently pursuing an engineering degree at the University of Technology of Compiègne.

First as a web developer and then as a web architect since 2012, Titouan has worked on Nginx intensively for PHP applications and Dockerized environments. Within the few years of his work, he has accumulated a lot of experience with Nginx and shares his experience in this book and in the related one, *Nginx High Performance*, *Packt Publishing*.

Valery Kholodkov is a seasoned IT professional with a decade of experience in creating, building, scaling, and maintaining industrial-grade web services, web applications, and mobile application backends. Throughout his career, he has worked for well-known brands such as Yandex, Booking.com, and AVG. He currently works as the CTO of QubiQ Digital, a consumer acquisition agency. Valery has a deep understanding of technology, and he is able to express its essence, advantages, and risks to a layman, which makes him an accomplished author and technical reviewer.

www.PacktPub.com

eBooks, discount offers, and more

Did you know that Packt offers eBook versions of every book published, with PDF and ePub files available? You can upgrade to the eBook version at www.PacktPub.com and as a print book customer, you are entitled to a discount on the eBook copy. Get in touch with us at customercare@packtpub.com for more details.

At www.PacktPub.com, you can also read a collection of free technical articles, sign up for a range of free newsletters and receive exclusive discounts and offers on Packt books and eBooks.

https://www2.packtpub.com/books/subscription/packtlib

Do you need instant solutions to your IT questions? PacktLib is Packt's online digital book library. Here, you can search, access, and read Packt's entire library of books.

Why subscribe?

- Fully searchable across every book published by Packt
- Copy and paste, print, and bookmark content
- On demand and accessible via a web browser

Table of Contents

Preface   **v**

Chapter 1: Searching for Problems in Nginx Configuration   **1**

  Introducing basic configuration syntax, directives, and testing   **2**
    Simple directives   3
    Multiline directives   3
    Include directive   4
  Testing Nginx configuration   **5**
    The default configuration directory layout   5
    A quick example of modifying the MIME types registry   7
    Default nginx.conf   9
    The http directive   10
  Common mistakes in configuration   **17**
    Semicolons and newlines   17
    File permissions   18
    Variables   19
    Regular expressions   19
  Summary   **21**

Chapter 2: Searching for Problems in Log Files   **23**

  Configuring Nginx logging   **23**
    Logging POST requests   32
    Conditional logging   35
    Logging big request bodies   36
  Creating infrastructure around logs   **37**
    Configuring log rotation   37
    Working with a lot of log data   40
    Reading logs   41
      Error log record   42
  Summary   **48**

Chapter 3: Troubleshooting Functionality   49

Processing a complain   50

Rolling back   51
    Keeping Nginx configuration under source control   52
Keeping a case journal   52
Performing the simplest test   53
Performing the Internet connection test   53
Testing the general HTTP response traffic   54
    Detecting a lying application   55
    Working around an integration failure   56
    Planning for more complete monitoring   60
Processing a situation of no traffic   61
    Restarting Nginx properly   67
Investigating lower than usual traffic   69

Summary   69

Chapter 4: Optimizing Website Performance   71

Why Nginx is so fast?   72
Optimizing individual upstreams   75

Optimizing static files   76
Optimizing PHP backends   76
Java backends   77
Optimizing Python and Ruby backends   78
Optimizing Perl backends   79

Using thread pools in Nginx   81
The caching layer of Nginx   82

Emitting caching headers   82
Caching in Nginx upstream modules   87
Caching static files   91

Replacing external redirects with internal ones   93
Summary   94

Chapter 5: Troubleshooting Rare Specific Problems   95

Security warnings   96

Domain name mismatch   97
Expired certificates   100
Insecure warnings for valid certificates   101
The mixed – content warning   102
    Building a secure proxy for the external content   106

Solving problems with cache   108
Obsolete pages and VirtualBox   110
Apache migration problems   110

Solving problems with WebSockets   **112**
Showing a file upload progress bar   **113**
Solving the problem of an idle upstream   **115**
Summary   **116**
Chapter 6: Monitoring Nginx   **117**
Using ngxtop   **118**
Getting statistics from http_stub_status   **120**
Monitoring Nginx with Munin   **125**
Configuring alerts   **128**
Getting more status data from Nginx   **130**
Using Nginx Plus alternatives   **135**
    nginx-module-vts   136
    Luameter   136
    nginx-lua-stats   136
    The upsteam_check module in tengine   137
    The requests/sec patch by Catap   138
    The Ustats module   138
Summary   **138**
Chapter 7: Going Forward with Nginx   **139**
System administration   **140**
    Linux/Unix operating system as a whole   140
    Modern Internet protocols   141
    Specific backend software used in your company   141
    Modern cloud platforms   142
    Automation   142
Software development   **143**
Summary   **144**
Appendix: Rare Nginx Error Messages   **145**
Index   **149**

Preface

You will learn how to notes problems before your boss calls you about some pages not loading. You will learn how to find those problems using logs and your usual Linux toolbox. You will also learn how to minimize the probability of problems happening again.

Nginx started as a web accelerator reverse proxy inside one of the big Russian web companies of the early 2000s. The main web server software was Apache 1.3, and it started to show architectural problems serving thousands of relatively slow clients using the old process-based model. Smart web engineers were already building two-tier systems of light frontends based on the `mod_proxy` Apache module or even used the squid caching proxy in the reverse proxy mode.

The early predecessor of Nginx was named `mod_accel`, and it was also implemented as an Apache module. The `mod_accel` module gained some popularity among the administrators of some of the busiest websites, but it is nothing compared with what Nginx later enjoyed. Both of them are built on the idea that the additional level of proxying on the server side of a busy website is a good thing, providing both the extra flexibility and separating the job of serving slow clients from the actual response generation.

Nginx took the idea of `mod_proxy` module to the extreme by being a self-sufficient separate HTTP server with a goal to solve the so-called C10K problem, that is, serving 10,000 concurrent connections. The numbers do not look impressive at all in 2016, but they did in 2007 when Nginx first claimed a significant share of 1% of the Web according to Netcraft.

Since that time, the share grew manifold while Nginx steadily gained new functionality and remained the ideal open source success story project with a single, talented developer devoting his genius to producing free quality software, which the whole Web could benefit from.

In 2011, a commercial enterprise named Nginx, Inc. was founded, which allowed even more freedom for the developers (now a team). The firm provides both support services and a special subscription-based extended version of the software named Nginx Plus. We will mention some of the Nginx Plus features in the sixth chapter.

In 2016, Nginx is a great tool many businesses are built upon. However, it is still just a tool which requires a master to show its full potential. If you want to understand what is going on in your web server, to be able to write correct Nginx configuration files and read Nginx logs, and if you want your web server to be very fast, you will have to become that master.

What this book covers

Chapter 1, Searching for Problems in Nginx Configuration, briefly describes the configuration language of Nginx and presents some of the corner cases and several techniques to search for problems.

Chapter 2, Searching for Problems in Log Files, describes the logging subsystem, log syntax, and what to look for when you troubleshoot. Nginx provides thorough logs of everything it does.

Chapter 3, Troubleshooting Functionality, the central chapter in this book, contains a list of steps you will make while investigating a problem. You will find the types of problems people generally encounter with their Nginx-powered web servers.

Chapter 4, Optimizing Website Performance, is dedicated to all things about performance. Starting with thorough explanation of the basic principles behind the Nginx event-driven processing model, it also touches on caching and even gives some advice on possible upstream optimization.

Chapter 5, Troubleshooting Rare Specific Problems, is devoted to studies of several real cases that you may face, from some of the simplest and easiest cases to fix to more problematic cases. The cases described might not be the most frequent, but they still provide valuable insight on the internals of the software and the methods of troubleshooting.

Chapter 6, Monitoring Nginx, is devoted to the abundance of tools available today that you may use for monitoring. No system is complete without good processes for the detection of emerging problems.

Chapter 7, Going Forward with Nginx, the short final chapter, provides a selection of directions you may choose for your further development as a specialist. The whole industry is very dynamic, and you should never settle.

Appendix, Rare Nginx Error Messages, provides a reference of interesting and not very common error messages that you might encounter in your log files.

What you need for this book

Although modern versions of Nginx support Windows, this configuration is not considered production-ready. Most of the examples in this book will work on your Windows machines, but we still recommend having a Linux or FreeBSD server for experiments.

Nginx itself is pretty stable, so any version released since 2013 will suffice. Some of the newer features are only available in more recent versions, and those cases are marked in the book. We always recommend running modern Nginx from the stable line in production. As of the start of the year 2016, it is 1.8.1.

Who this book is for

The book is for technical specialists who already use Nginx to serve web pages for their users. Whether you are an experienced system administrator or a new professional, this book will help you do your job in the most efficient way.

Conventions

In this book, you will find a number of text styles that distinguish between different kinds of information. Here are some examples of these styles and an explanation of their meaning.

Code words in text, database table names, folder names, filenames, file extensions, pathnames, dummy URLs, user input, and Twitter handles are shown as follows: "The `error_page` directive installs a handler for an HTTP error based on the famous HTTP status codes."

A block of code is set as follows:

```
...
simple_command 4 "two";
# another_simple_command 0;

special_context {
    some_special_command /new/path;
    multiline_directive param {
        1 2 3 5 8 13;
    }
    include common_parameters;
}
...
```

When we wish to draw your attention to a particular part of a code block, the relevant lines or items are set in bold:

```
Cache-Control:"max-age=1800"
Content-Encoding:"gzip"
Content-Type:"text/html; charset=UTF-8"
Date:"Sun, 10 Oct 2015 13:42:34 GMT"
Expires:"Sun, 10 Oct 2015 14:12:34 GMT"
Server:"nginx"
X-Cache:"EXPIRED"
```

Any command-line input or output is written as follows:

```
% sudo nginx -t
nginx: [emerg] unexpected end of file, expecting "}" in
/etc/nginx/nginx.conf:1
nginx: configuration file /etc/nginx/nginx.conf test failed
```

New terms and **important words** are shown in bold. Words that you see on the screen, for example, in menus or dialog boxes, appear in the text like this: "You should have a way to reboot an otherwise unreachable server; every sane modern hosting provider has it, whether in the form of a simple menu item **Reboot**, such as in Amazon EC2 or a whole IPMI console access."

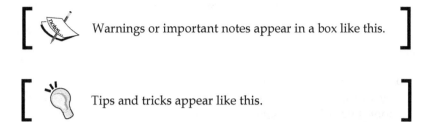

Warnings or important notes appear in a box like this.

Tips and tricks appear like this.

Reader feedback

Feedback from our readers is always welcome. Let us know what you think about this book—what you liked or disliked. Reader feedback is important for us as it helps us develop titles that you will really get the most out of.

To send us general feedback, simply e-mail feedback@packtpub.com, and mention the book's title in the subject of your message.

If there is a topic that you have expertise in and you are interested in either writing or contributing to a book, see our author guide at www.packtpub.com/authors.

Customer support

Now that you are the proud owner of a Packt book, we have a number of things to help you to get the most from your purchase.

Downloading the example code

You can download the example code files for this book from your account at http://www.packtpub.com. If you purchased this book elsewhere, you can visit http://www.packtpub.com/support and register to have the files e-mailed directly to you.

You can download the code files by following these steps:

1. Log in or register to our website using your e-mail address and password.
2. Hover the mouse pointer on the **SUPPORT** tab at the top.
3. Click on **Code Downloads & Errata**.
4. Enter the name of the book in the **Search** box.

5. Select the book for which you're looking to download the code files.

6. Choose from the drop-down menu where you purchased this book from.

7. Click on **Code Download**.

You can also download the code files by clicking on the **Code Files** button on the book's webpage at the Packt Publishing website. This page can be accessed by entering the book's name in the **Search** box. Please note that you need to be logged in to your Packt account.

Once the file is downloaded, please make sure that you unzip or extract the folder using the latest version of:

- WinRAR / 7-Zip for Windows
- Zipeg / iZip / UnRarX for Mac
- 7-Zip / PeaZip for Linux

Downloading the color images of this book

We also provide you with a PDF file that has color images of the screenshots/diagrams used in this book. The color images will help you better understand the changes in the output. You can download this file from `https://www.packtpub.com/sites/default/files/downloads/NginxTroubleshooting_ColorImages.pdf`.

Errata

Although we have taken every care to ensure the accuracy of our content, mistakes do happen. If you find a mistake in one of our books—maybe a mistake in the text or the code—we would be grateful if you could report this to us. By doing so, you can save other readers from frustration and help us improve subsequent versions of this book. If you find any errata, please report them by visiting `http://www.packtpub.com/submit-errata`, selecting your book, clicking on the **Errata Submission Form** link, and entering the details of your errata. Once your errata are verified, your submission will be accepted and the errata will be uploaded to our website or added to any list of existing errata under the Errata section of that title.

To view the previously submitted errata, go to `https://www.packtpub.com/books/content/support` and enter the name of the book in the search field. The required information will appear under the **Errata** section.

Piracy

Piracy of copyrighted material on the Internet is an ongoing problem across all media. At Packt, we take the protection of our copyright and licenses very seriously. If you come across any illegal copies of our works in any form on the Internet, please provide us with the location address or website name immediately so that we can pursue a remedy.

Please contact us at copyright@packtpub.com with a link to the suspected pirated material.

We appreciate your help in protecting our authors and our ability to bring you valuable content.

Questions

If you have a problem with any aspect of this book, you can contact us at questions@packtpub.com, and we will do our best to address the problem.

1
Searching for Problems in Nginx Configuration

Nginx is a complex piece of software that will help you implement your own part of the World Wide Web—one of the killer applications of the Internet as a whole. Although seeming to be simple, the Web and the underlying HTTP have a lot of intricate details that may require special attention. Nginx gives you the power to pay that attention to those details by means of the extensive configuration language. Following the grand UNIX tradition of human-readable and writable text configuration files, Nginx expects a certain level of understanding and zeal from you so that it can serve in the best way possible. It also means that there is freedom and huge potential for mistakes.

The main goal of this chapter is to lead you through the way Nginx is configured and show you some of the areas that are prone to errors.

You will find further:

- Configuration syntax with description and examples
- Description of all files in the default configuration bundled with Nginx
- Some mistakes you could make with examples from the default configuration and techniques to avoid them

Introducing basic configuration syntax, directives, and testing

Igor Sysoev, the principal author of Nginx, said, on several occasions, that he designed the Nginx configuration language in such a way that writing the configuration should not feel like programming, or actual coding. For a long time, he himself worked as a professional system administrator for several relatively big websites in Russia. He understood perfectly that the goal of a website administrator is not to end up with beautiful, elegant configurations or to have at one's disposal every imaginable function for all possible situations no matter how rare they are. The goal is to be able to declaratively describe the business requirements, to formulate which behavior is needed without delving into how that could be achieved in software. One interesting example of quite the opposite idea in language design is the Lighttpd configuration language, but that's out of the scope of this book.

This is what we have now—a simple declarative language inspired by Apache's one but without all the XML-like tags. Open the default `nginx.conf` file to see what Nginx configuration looks like. Some distributions contain their own modifications to the default file. We will use the one from the original tarball available at `http://nginx.org/download/nginx-1.9.12.tar.gz`. What follows is a quick syntax introduction using parts of that file as examples. You might find it too obvious but bear with us; even the most experienced reader will do good to refresh his or her memory.

Let us look at the very beginning of the file. Lines starting with # are comments, and they are ignored. *Commenting out* is a very common technique to make Nginx ignore a part of configuration. The topmost line in default Nginx configuration file (as of version 1.9.12) is actually commented out:

```
...
#user   nobody;
...
```

One easy way to comment out a block of lines in vim is highlighting them visually with *Shift-V* and then issuing the `:s/^/#/` ex command. In Emacs, just select a region and then press *M-;*.

Nonempty noncommented lines in Nginx configuration are of the two following types.

Simple directives

Simple directives consist of a command word followed by a number of parameters and a semicolon. For example (see at the top of the default `nginx.conf` file):

```
...
worker_processes   1;
...
```

Nothing to worry about here. People having too much experience with modern scripting languages, such as Python and Ruby, tend to forget the semicolon; we advise you to make sure that you add it.

The parameters mentioned here can be either constant values (numbers or strings, which does not matter, they are all parsed in the same way at this level) or they may contain variables. Variables in Nginx are the `$dollar_prefixed` identifiers that are replaced with some actual value at runtime. For example, there are variables containing data from an HTTP request, and you can modify website behavior depending on their values or just log them.

A very good example of variables in the default `nginx.conf` file is this:

```
...
#log_format   main  '$remote_addr - $remote_user [$time_local]
"$request" '
#                     '$status $body_bytes_sent "$http_referer" '
#                     '"$http_user_agent" "$http_x_forwarded_for"';
...
```

This directive creates a log format by constructing a template for each line of the log. It uses a number of variables available during the request/response cycle.

Multiline directives

Multiline directives are simple directives with a BUT. Instead of a semicolon in the end, there is a block enclosed in braces { ... }. And here *instead* is meant literally. You don't put semicolons after closing braces. Those of you with just enough experience with more traditional C-like syntax programming languages will find this very natural.

Here is an example of the very first multiline directive in the default Nginx 1.9.12 `nginx.conf` file:

```
events {
    worker_connections  1024;
}
```

Now, this is an `events` directive, which does not have any parameters, and it contains a block instead of a semicolon. Because of these blocks, multiline directives are also named "block directives". Blocks contain various kinds of content, but one of the most important and interesting blocks is the one containing other directives — both simple and multiline.

In the previous example, the block of the `events` directive contains a simple `worker_connections` directive.

Multiline directives that allow other directives inside their blocks are named "contexts". They introduce new context for the enclosed, inner part of the configuration.

Most of the multiline directives are actually contexts — from the most popular, such as `server` or `location`, to the most obscure, such as `limit_except`. An example of a multiline directive that is not a context is `types`, which introduces the relation between file extensions and the so-called **Multipurpose Internet Mail Extensions** (**MIME**) types. We will look at `types` later in this chapter.

Contexts are very important. They are scopes and topics of the directives that are inside. If a command is not included in any multiline directive block, then it is considered part of the special context named "main" with the widest scope. Directives in this context affect the whole Nginx application. Other contexts are all either inside "main" or even deeper below, and the commands that are contained within those contexts have narrower scopes and affect only parts of the whole.

Include directive

We will not describe actual directives here except for one of them. It is the `include` directive, a special dear to the hearts of all sysadmins who scale their work to many websites, servers, or just URLs. It is a very simple block-level "package management tool" if we are allowed to use more programming terminology. This simple directive has one parameter, that is, a filename or a wild card (UNIX glob-style) matching a number of files. During processing, this directive is replaced by the contents of the files it refers to. A quick example (from the default `nginx.conf` file):

```
...
include fastcgi_params;
...
```

We won't offend you by spending more time on explaining `include`. What we need to add is that included files have to be fully correct syntactically. You cannot have half of a command in one file and then include the rest from another.

So, this is it, the whole syntax is described. Let us show you a fictional piece of configuration that demonstrates everything but does not actually work because it contains nonexistent directives (or maybe those are from some future version of Nginx):

```
...
simple_command 4 "two";
# another_simple_command 0;

special_context {
    some_special_command /new/path;
    multiline_directive param {
        1 2 3 5 8 13;
    }
    include common_parameters;
}
...
```

Testing Nginx configuration

There is a very handy tool in the Nginx kit, a syntax checker for the configuration files. It is built into the main Nginx executable application and invoked by using the -t command-line switch as follows:

```
...
% nginx -t
nginx: the configuration file /etc/nginx/nginx.conf syntax is ok
nginx: configuration file /etc/nginx/nginx.conf test is successful
...
```

The command nginx -t tries to check your configuration quite thoroughly. For example, it will check all the included files and try to access all the auxiliary files like logs or pids to warn you about their nonexistence or insufficient permissions. You will become a better Nginx administrator if you acquire a habit of frequently running nginx -t.

The default configuration directory layout

We will now run through the entire configuration that you get bundled with Nginx by default. Some of it is a good example from which you will start writing your own. Some of it is just a sign of Nginx age. Again, we use the original tarball for the 1.9.12 version that is available on the official Nginx website.

This is a list of files inside the `conf` folder of the Nginx source archive:

```
...
% ls
fastcgi.conf      koi-utf  mime.types  scgi_params   win-utf
fastcgi_params    koi-win  nginx.conf  uwsgi_params
...
```

The `nginx.conf` is the main file, the one everything starts with. All other files are either included from `nginx.conf` or not used at all. Actually, `nginx.conf` is the only configuration file that is required by Nginx code (and you can override even that by using `-c` command-line switch). We will discuss its content a little bit later.

A pair of `fastcgi.conf` and `fastcgi_params` files contains almost the same list of simple commands configuring the Nginx FastCGI client. FastCGI, being an interface to run web applications behind Nginx, is not turned on by default. These two files are provided as examples (one of them is even included with the `include` command from a commented section of the `nginx.conf` file).

Three files with enigmatic names `koi-utf`, `koi-win`, and `win-utf` are character maps to convert between different ways to encode Cyrillic characters in electronic documents. And Cyrillic is, of course, the script used for Russian and several other languages. In the old days of the first Internet hosts in Russia, there was a dispute on which way to encode Russian letters in documents. You can read about different Cyrillic charsets/encodings at `http://czyborra.com/charsets/cyrillic. html`. Several of them got popular, and web servers had to include functionality of converting documents on the fly in the case that a client browser requested a different encoding from what was used by the server. There was also a whole fork of Apache Web Server that had this functionality built in. Nginx had to do the same to stand a chance against Apache. And now, more than 10 years later, we still have these re-encoding files that are deeply obsolete as the global **World Wide Web** continues to move towards UTF-8 as the one universal encoding for all human languages. You won't ever use these `koi-utf`, `koi-win`, and `win-utf` files unless you support a very old website for Russian-speaking visitors.

The file named `mime.types` is used by default. You can see that it is included from the main `nginx.conf`, and you better leave it that way. "MIME types" is a registry of different types of information in files.

They have their origin in some of the email standards (hence, the MIME name) but are used everywhere, including the Web. Let's look inside `mime.types`:

```
...
types {
    text/html                          html htm shtml;
    text/css                           css;
    text/xml                           xml;
    image/gif                          gif;
...
```

Because it is included from `nginx.conf`, it should have a proper Nginx configuration language syntax. That's right, it contains a single multiline directive `types`, which is not a context (as described in the previous section). Its block is a list of pairs, each being a mapping from one MIME type to a list of file extensions. This mapping is used to mark static files served by Nginx as having a particular MIME (or content) type. According to the quoted segment, the files `common.css` and `new.css` will get the type `text/css`, whereas `index.shtml` will be `text/html`, and so on and so forth; it is really easy.

A quick example of modifying the MIME types registry

Sometimes, you will add things to this registry. Let's try to do this now and demonstrate an introduction of a simple mistake and the workflow to find and fix it.

Your website will host calendars for your colleagues. A calendar is a file in the iCalendar format generated by a third-party application and saved to a file with `.ics` extension. There is nothing about `ics` in the default `mime.types`, and because of this, your Nginx instance will serve these files with the default `application/octet-stream` MIME type, which basically means "it is a bunch of octets (bytes) and I don't have the faintest idea of what they mean". Suppose that the new calendar application your colleagues use require proper iCalendar-typed HTTP responses. This means that you have to add this `text/calendar` type into your `mime.types` file.

You open `mime.types` in your editor and add this line to the very end (not in the middle, not to the start, but the end is important for the sake of this experiment) of the file:

```
...
text/calendar ics
...
```

You then run `nginx -t` because you are a good Nginx administrator:

```
...
nginx: [emerg] unexpected end of file, expecting ";" or "}" in
/etc/nginx/mime.types:91
nginx: configuration file /etc/nginx/nginx.conf test failed
...
```

Bam. Nginx is smart enough to tell you what you need to fix; this line does not look like either a simple or a multiline directive. Let's add the semicolon:

```
...
text/calendar ics;
...
```

```
...
nginx: [emerg] unknown directive "text/calendar" in
/etc/nginx/mime.types:90
nginx: configuration file /etc/nginx/nginx.conf test failed
...
```

Now this is more obscure. What you should do here is understand that this line is not a separate standalone directive. It is a part of the big `types` multiline (the rare, non-context one) directive; therefore, it should be moved into the block.

Change the tail of the `mime.types` from this:

```
}
text/calendar ics;
```

The preceding code should look as follows:

```
text/calendar ics;
}
```

It is done by swapping the last two meaningful lines:

```
nginx: the configuration file /etc/nginx/nginx.conf syntax is ok
nginx: configuration file /etc/nginx/nginx.conf test is successful
```

Congratulations, you just enabled a new business process for your company involving mobile workforce.

Two last default configuration files are `scgi_params` and `uwsgi_params`. Those two are the counterparts for the `fastcgi_params`, setting up two alternative methods of running web application on your web servers (SCGI and UWSGI, respectively, as you guessed). You will use them if and when your application developers will bring you applications written with these interfaces in mind.

Default nginx.conf

Now, let's dig deeper into the main configuration file `nginx.conf`. In its default form that you see inside the tarball, it is rather empty and useless. At the same time, it is always what you use as a starting point when writing your own configuration, and it can also be used as a demonstration of some common troubles that people inflict on themselves. Going over each directive is not needed, so only those that are good to demonstrate a technique or a common place of errors will be included in this section:

```
...
#user nobody;
...
```

This directive specifies the name of the UNIX user that Nginx processes will run as. Commenting out pieces of configuration is a common documentation technique. It shows the default values and removing the comment character is safe. Nginx will complain if you try to run it as a nonexistent user. As a general rule, you should either trust your package vendor and not change the default or use an account with the least permissions possible.

```
...
#error_log  logs/error.log;
#error_log  logs/error.log  notice;
#error_log  logs/error.log  info;

#pid        logs/nginx.pid;
...
```

These lines specify some default filenames. The three `error_log` directives are an example of yet another technique: providing several variants as comments so that you can uncomment the one you prefer. These three differ by the level of detail that goes into the error log. There is a whole chapter about logs as those are definitely the first and foremost debugging and troubleshooting tool available for any Nginx administrator.

The `pid` directive allows you to change the filename where pid of the main Nginx process will be stored. You rarely have to change this.

Note that these directives use relative paths in these examples, but this is not required. They could also use absolute paths (starting with /). The `error_log` directive provides two other ways of logging besides simple files, which you will see later.

```
...
events {
    worker_connections  1024;
}
...
```

This is our first context and a confusing one. `events` is not used to narrow the scope of directives inside it. Most of those directives cannot be used in any other context except `events`. This is used as a logical grouping mechanism for many parameters that configure the way Nginx responds to activity on the network. These are very general words, but they fit the purpose. Think of `events` as a fancy historical way of marking a group of parameters that are close to one another.

The `worker_connections` directive specifies the maximum number of all network connections each worker process will have. It may be a source of strange mistakes. You should remember that this limit includes both the client connections between Nginx and your user's browsers and the `server` connections that Nginx will have to open for your backend web application code (unless you only serve static files).

The http directive

```
...
http {
    include       mime.types;
    default_type  application/octet-stream;
...
```

Here we go, `http` marks the start of a huge context that usually spans several files (via nested includes) and groups all the configuration parameters that concern the web part of Nginx. You might feel that this sounds a lot like `events`, but it is actually a very valid context requiring a separate directive because Nginx can work not only as an HTTP server but also serve some other protocols, for example, IMAP and POP3. It is an infrequent use case, to put it mildly, and we won't spend our time on it, but it shows a very legitimate reason to have a special scope for all HTTP options.

You probably know what the first two directives inside `http` do. Never change the default MIME type. Many web clients use this particular type as an indication of a file that needs to be saved on the client computer as an opaque blob of data, and it is a good idea for all the unknown files.

```
    . . .
    #log_format   main   '$remote_addr - $remote_user [$time_local]
"$request" '
    #                       '$status $body_bytes_sent "$http_referer" '
    #                       '"$http_user_agent"
"$http_x_forwarded_for"';

    #access_log  logs/access.log   main;
    . . .
```

These two directives specify logging of all requests, both successful and unsuccessful, for the reason of tracing and statistics. The first directive creates a log format and the second initiates logging to a specific file according to the mentioned format. It is a very powerful mechanism that gets special attention later in this book. Then we have the following code:

```
    . . .
    sendfile         on;
    #tcp_nopush      on;

    #keepalive_timeout   0;
    keepalive_timeout   65;

    #gzip  on;
    . . .
```

The first and the second of these turn on certain networking features of the HTTP support. `sendfile` is a syscall that allows copying of bytes from a file to a socket by the OS kernel itself, sometimes using "zero copy" semantics. It is always safe to leave it on unless you have very little memory — there were reports that sometimes `sendfile` boxes may work unreliably on servers with little memory. `tcp_nopush` is an option that makes sense only in the presence of `sendfile on`. It allows you to optimize a number of network packets that a `sendfile-d` file gets sent in. `keepalive` is a feature of modern HTTP — the browser (on any other client) may choose not to close a connection to a server right away but to keep it open just in case there will be a need to talk to the same server again very soon. For many modern web pages, consisting of hundreds of objects, this could help a lot, especially on HTTPS, where the cost of opening a new connection is higher. `keepalive` timeout is a period in seconds that Nginx will not drop open connections to clients. Tweaking the default value of 75 will rarely affect performance. You can try if you know something special about your clients, but usually people either leave the default timeout or turn the `keepalive` off altogether by setting the timeout to zero.

There are a (big) number of compression algorithms much better than the LZW of the traditional gzip, but gzip is most widely available among servers and clients on the web, providing good enough compression for texts with very little cost. `gzip on` will turn on automatic compression of data on the fly between Nginx and its clients, that is, those which announce support for gzipped server responses, of course. There are still browsers in the wild that do not support gzip properly. See the description of the `gzip_disable` directive in the Nginx documentation at `http://nginx.org/en/docs/http/ngx_http_gzip_module.html#gzip_disable`. It might be a source of problems, but only if you have some really odd users either with weird special-case client software or from the past.

```
    . . .
    server {
        listen          80;
        server_name     localhost;
    . . .
```

Now we have another multiline context directive inside `http`. It is a famous `server` directive that configures a single web server object with a hostname and a TCP port to listen on. Those two are the top-most directives inside this `server`. The first, `listen` has a much more complex syntax than just a port number, and we will not describe it here. The second one has a simple syntax, but some complex rules of matching that are also better described in the online documentation. It will be sufficient to say that these two provide a way of choosing the right server to process an incoming HTTP request. The most useful is the `server_name` in its simplest form; it just contains a hostname in the form of DNS domain and it will be matched against the name that browser sent in the `Host:` header which, in turn, is just the host name part of the URL.

```
    . . .
        #charset koi8-r;
    . . .
```

This is a way to indicate the charset (encoding) of the documents you serve to the browsers. It is set by default to the special value `off` and not the good old `koi8-r` from RFC1489. Nowadays, your best bet is specifying `utf8` here or just leaving it off. If you specify a charset that does not correspond to the actual charset of your documents, you will get troubles.

```
    . . .
        #access_log  logs/host.access.log  main;
    . . .
```

Here is an interesting example of using a directive inside a narrowing context. Remember that we already discussed `access_log` one level higher, inside the `http` directive. This one will turn on logging of requests to this particular server only. It is a good habit to include the name of the server in the name of its access log. So, replace `host` with something very similar to your `server_name`.

```
. . .
        location / {
            root    html;
            index   index.html index.htm;
        }
. . .
```

Again, we see a multiline directive introducing a context for a number of URLs on this particular server. `location /` will match all the requests unless there is a more specific location on the same level. The rules to choose the correct location block to process an incoming request are quite complex, but simple cases could be described with simple words.

The `index` directive specifies the way to process URLs that correspond to a local folder. In this case, Nginx seeks the first existing file from the list in this directive. Serving either an `index.html` or `index.htm` for such URLs is a very old convention; you shouldn't break it unless you know what you are doing.

By the way, `index.htm` without the last `l` is an artifact of the old Microsoft filesystems that allowed three or less characters in the filename extension. Nginx never worked on Microsoft systems with such limitations, but files ending in `htm` instead of `html` still linger around.

```
. . .
        #error_page  404               /404.html;

        # redirect server error pages to the static page /50x.html
        #
        error_page   500 502 503 504   /50x.html;
        location = /50x.html {
            root    html;
        }
. . .
```

These directives set up the way errors are reported to the user. You, as the webmaster, will most certainly rely on your logs but just in case something happened, your users should not be left in dark. The `error_page` directive installs a handler for an HTTP error based on the famous HTTP status codes. The first example (commented) tells Nginx that in case it encounters a 404 (not found) error, it should not report it to the user as a real 404 error but instead initiate the subrequest to the `/404.html` location, render the results, and present them in the response to the original user request.

By the way, one of the most embarrassing mistakes you could make with Apache web server is to provide a 404 handler that raises another 404 error. Remember these?

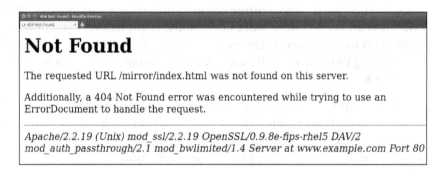

Nginx will not show this type of detail to users, but they will still see some very ugly error messages:

The `location = /50x.html` looks suspiciously similar to the one we discussed earlier. The only important difference is the = character that means "exact match". The whole matching algorithm is a complete topic in itself, but here you should definitely remember that = means "process requests for this and only this URL, do not treat it as a prefix that could match longer URLs".

```
    ...
        # proxy the PHP scripts to Apache listening on
    127.0.0.1:80
```

```
        #
        #location ~ \.php$ {
        #    proxy_pass    http://127.0.0.1;
        #}

        # pass the PHP scripts to FastCGI server listening on
127.0.0.1:9000
        #
        #location ~ \.php$ {
        #    root           html;
        #    fastcgi_pass   127.0.0.1:9000;
        #    fastcgi_index  index.php;
        #    fastcgi_param  SCRIPT_FILENAME
/scripts$fastcgi_script_name;
        #    include        fastcgi_params;
        #}
    ...
```

This is a big commented chunk of options all about the same – processing PHP scripts using two different strategies. Nginx, as you know, does not try to be everything, and it especially tries to never be an application server. The first location directive sets up proxying to another local PHP server, probably Apache with mod_php.

> Pay attention to the ~ character in location. It turns on regular expressions engine for the matching of the URLs, hence the escaped . and the $ in the end. Nginx regular expressions use the common syntax originating from the first grep and ed programs written in the late 1960s. They are implemented with the PCRE library. See the PCRE documentation for the comprehensive description of the language at http://www.pcre.org/original/doc/html/ pcrepattern.html.

The second block talks to a FastCGI server running locally on the 9000 port instead of HTTP proxying. It is a bit more modern way of running PHP, but it also requires a lot of parameters (see included file) as compared with the very simple and humble HTTP.

```
    ...
        # deny access to .htaccess files, if Apache's document
root
        # concurs with Nginx's one
        #
```

```
        #location ~ /\.ht {
        #    deny  all;
        #}
    . . .
```

The last part of the server block under discussion introduces **Access Control Lists (ACLs)**, in a `location` with a regular expression. The note in the comment is a curious one. There is a tradition of "bolting" Nginx onto an existing Apache installation so that Nginx would serve all the static files itself while proxying more complex, dynamic URLs to the downstream Apache. This kind of setup is definitely not recommended, but you have probably seen or even inherited one. Nginx itself does not support the local `.htaccess` files but has to protect those files left from Apache because they could contain sensitive information.

And the final server multiline directive is an example of a secure server serving HTTPS:

```
    . . .
        # HTTPS server
        #
        #server {
        #    listen        443 ssl;
        #    server_name  localhost;

        #    ssl_certificate       cert.pem;
        #    ssl_certificate_key  cert.key;

        #    ssl_session_cache     shared:SSL:1m;
        #    ssl_session_timeout  5m;

        #    ssl_ciphers  HIGH:!aNULL:!MD5;
        #    ssl_prefer_server_ciphers  on;

        #    location / {
        #        root    html;
        #        index  index.html index.htm;
        #    }
        #}
    . . .
```

Besides a bunch of simple `ssl_` directives in the middle, the important thing to note is `listen 443 ssl`, which enables HTTPS (basically, HTTPS is HTTP over SSL on the TCP port `443`). We talk about HTTPS in *Chapter 3, Troubleshooting Functionality* of this book.

Common mistakes in configuration

Reading default configuration files may turn out interesting and educating, but more useful thing is, of course, looking at examples of configuration that is actually used in production. We will now look at some common mistakes that happen during the configuration of Nginx.

If you don't see something that has happened to you and you need help immediately, by all means skip and browse the rest of the book. There are a lot more examples throughout the chapters grouped by the nature of the problem or the effects it has.

Semicolons and newlines

One common feature of truly great software is forgiving. Nginx will understand and autocorrect some syntax violations when the result is unambiguous. For example, if your hands insist on enclosing values in quotes—you can actually do this.

This is completely legal and works okay:

```
. . .
user "nobody" 'www-data';
worker_processes '2';
. . .
```

On the other hand, here is a case when Nginx will not allow you to leave a stray, unneeded semicolon although it does not introduce any ambiguity:

```
. . .
events {
    worker_connections 768;
    # multi_accept on;
};
. . .
```

```
% sudo nginx -t
nginx: [emerg] unexpected ";" in /etc/nginx/nginx.conf:13
nginx: configuration file /etc/nginx/nginx.conf test failed
```

The author once had a configuration file saved in the older Mac format, that is, with <CR> as the newline separator. This is a format used on pre-OS X Apple operating systems. Text editors and pagers work around this rare curiosity, and you will have a hard time noticing anything unusual. Nginx could not split the file into lines at all:

```
% sudo nginx -t
```

```
nginx: [emerg] unexpected end of file, expecting "}" in
/etc/nginx/nginx.conf:1
```

```
nginx: configuration file /etc/nginx/nginx.conf test failed
```

The way to fix it is to convert newlines from <CR> to <LF> or to <CR><LF>. The easiest method, using `tr` from the Unix/Linux command line, looks like this:

```
% tr '\r' '\n' < /etc/nginx/nginx.conf > /tmp/nginx.conf
```

(After this, check it manually and replace the old file with `mv`.)

File permissions

Have you noticed that we run `nginx -t` with `sudo`? Let us try without `sudo` and see what happens:

It is actually quite interesting. Nginx reported that the syntax of the file is okay, but then it decided to dig deeper and check not only the syntax but also the availability of some features mentioned in the configuration. First, it complained about not being able to change the effective user under whose permissions all the worker processes should run. Do you remember the `user` directive? It also tried to open both the main server-wide error log and the `pid` file that is rewritten on each restart of Nginx. Both of them are not available for writing from the main working account (and they should not be, of course). That is why sudo is needed when running `nginx -t`.

Variables

Here is another example of a simple syntax error that might bite you once or twice in your career. Do you remember variables that we discussed several pages before? Nginx uses `$syntax` that is very familiar to everyone with the UNIX shell, awk, Perl, or PHP programming experience. Still, it is very easy to miss the dollar character and Nginx will not notice that because a variable will just turn into a simple string constant.

When you set up your Nginx as a proxy for another web server (such configuration is traditionally named "reverse accelerator", but less and less often so in recent times), you will quickly find that all client connections to your backend server come from the same IP address, the address of your Nginx host. The reason is obvious, but once you have some backend logic depending on getting the actual client address, you will need to work around this limitation of proxying. A common practice is to include an additional HTTP request header on all requests from Nginx to the backend. Here is how you do that:

```
...
proxy_set_header X-Real-IP $remote_addr;
...
```

The application will have to check for this header, and only in its absence use the actual client IP address from the socket. Now, imagine losing that dollar sign in the beginning of `$remote_addr`. Suddenly, your Nginx will add a very strange header of `X-Real-IP: remote_addr` to all requests. `nginx -t` won't be able to detect this. Your backend application might blow up in case there is a strict IP address parser or, and this is ironically worse, it might skip the unparsable IP address of `remote_addr` and default to the actual address of your Nginx never ever reporting this to any logs. You will end up with a working configuration that silently loses valuable information! Depending on luck, this could be in production for months before someone notices that some fresh "rate-limiting by IP" feature of the application starts to affect all users at once!

Ah, the horrors!

Regular expressions

Let us get to something less destructive. Many Nginx directives make use of regular expressions. You should be familiar with them. If not, we would recommend stopping your work as soon as possible and leaving for a bookstore. Regular expressions are considered by many IT practitioners to be the single most important technology or skill for everyday use after fast typing.

Most often, you will see regexps in `location` multiline directive. Besides this, they are very useful (and sometimes unavoidable) in URL rewriting and hostname matching. Regular expressions are a mini-language that uses several characters as metacharacters to construct patterns from strings. Those patterns cover sets of strings (very often infinite sets); the process of checking whether a particular string is contained in the set corresponding to a pattern is named matching. This is a simple regexp from the default `nginx.conf` file:

```
. . .
#location ~ \.php$ {
#     proxy_pass   http://127.0.0.1;
#}
. . .
```

The tilde after the `location` command word means that what follows is a regular expression to match against incoming URLs. `\.php$` covers an infinite set of all strings in the universe that have these exact four characters in the very end: `.php`. The backslash before the dot cancels the metavalue of the dot, which is "any character". The dollar sign is a metacharacter that matches the very end of a string.

How many ways are there to make a mistake in that expression? A lot. A very big number. Will `nginx -t` point out those errors? Most probably, no, unless you happen to make the whole directive somehow invalid and due to the very expressive nature of the mini-language, almost all character combinations are valid. Let's try some:

```
. . .
        location ~ \.php {
. . .
```

Did you notice? Right, no dollar, again as in the variable example shown previously. This is perfectly valid. It will also pass most tests because this regexp covers an even larger infinite set of all strings that have `.php` as a substring, not necessarily in the end. What could possibly go wrong? Well, first, you could get a request for the URL that looks like `"/mirrors/www.phpworld.example.com/index.html"` and blow up. And second, matching by comparing the last 4 characters is logically much simpler than searching the whole buffer for the substring. This could have performance effects, however, small.

Let's skip the backslash instead:

```
. . .
        location ~ .php$ {
. . .
```

Evil. This will also pass the tests but again, the set of matching strings grew. Now the dot before the php is not literal. It is a metadot meaning any character. You have to be lucky to get something like /download/version-for-php, but once you get this, the location will match. You have a time bomb.

Now, let's drop the tilde:

```
    . . .
            location \.php$ {
    . . .
```

Do you like our game by the way? You should already predict what will happen and how to fix it, that is, if you do like it and are starting to think like an Nginx instance.

The missing tilde will turn this location directive into its simplest form — no regular expressions whatsoever. The string \.php$ is interpreted as a prefix to search for in all incoming URLs, together with the backslash and the dollar. Will this location block ever process a single request? We don't know. One important thing here is that nginx -t still does not have anything to say about this directive. It is still valid syntactically.

Summary

In this chapter, you refreshed your knowledge of how exactly Nginx is configured. We showed how the language looks and what some common pitfalls are when writing it. Some of you learned a thing or two about the mysterious files that Nginx authors included in the default conf folder; some will never ever miss a semicolon again. Run nginx -t often, but never blindly rely on it saying everything is okay.

The next chapter is devoted to reading and configuring logging mechanisms inside Nginx.

2
Searching for Problems
in Log Files

Nginx really is a breakthrough technology powering a great part of modern Web. And as with all great technologies, it stands on the shoulders of giants. Nginx would not be possible without Apache. One very important Unix tradition that Nginx embraces fully is thorough logging.

Logs are what you turn to the moment there is a problem with your Nginx instance. For a daemon, there are not really many ways to communicate its state to the administrator in a simple, reliable, and guaranteed to work way other than logs.

You will find the following topics in this chapter:

- A comprehensive description of how Nginx logging is configured and what mistakes could be made in the configuration
- A special section on how to log POST request bodies
- A section on how log rotation works and why there is some potential for problems
- A series of real-life error records from logs with analysis

Configuring Nginx logging

There are two types of logs that Nginx may write. One could also say that there are infinite types because of the `log_format` directive that allows you to create your own types of logs.

To refresh your memory about what directives are used to configure Nginx logging, here they are:

- The `error_log` directive configures the logging of exceptional events that the developers of Nginx consider worth noting. Usually, this is all kinds of errors.

  The format of the directive is this:

  ```
  error_log <destination> <log level>;
  ```

The first parameter is usually a path to the file with the log. Recent versions of Nginx starting with 1.7.1 also support logging via syslog, to a local or remote syslog server. There is also a rarely used misnamed special value `stderr`, which, by the way, does not redirect logging to `stderr` (the third standard `stdio` stream or `&2` in shell terms) because it does not make much sense to log to `stderr` from a daemon — daemonization involves closing all standard file descriptors. The `stderr` value means "log into the file that was configured during compilation time" and that depends on the package or even the OS distribution you use. You will mostly want to specify an actual file instead of `stderr` just to be sure where it ends. By the way, to make things more confusing, there is a way to specify logging to actual `stderr` during compile time. It is not very useful for daemons; you will not probably ever use it.

You often want several error logs. Remember that in *Chapter 1, Searching for Problems in Nginx Configuration*, we discussed multiline configuration directives named contexts. They provide a topic, that is, a narrow scope for the directives inside them. You may (and that is usually a very good idea) have different log files in different contexts. And using `stderr` prevents that because everything will get written to the same place.

The `log level` parameter of the `error_log` directive is a way of specifying a threshold of severity of events that end up in the log. Most of the time, you will want to set this to `warn`, but feel free to increase up to `debug` whenever you have a reproducible problem that you want more information about.

The `debug` level requires a special compile-time switch. The reason for this is that `debug` logging makes some performance compromises and the code for it should not be included in production systems, ideally. Unless Nginx is really your bottleneck (a rare situation), you may safely use `--with-debug` when compiling Nginx. See a little more about it at `http://nginx.org/en/docs/debugging_log.html`.

- The other logging directive is `access_log`. And it includes much more functionality than `error_log` and also more potential for mistakes. Let's look at it more closely.

This is how access logs are configured:

```
access_log <destination> <log format> <misc arguments>
```

The idea of access log is to have a journal of all request-response pairs processed by Nginx. As opposed to the error log, the records in access logs have a thoroughly specified format, usually a chain of whitespace-delimited values that contain some information about the current request-response pair or general state of Nginx. All access log records have this format. Access logs and error logs work together. In case Nginx has something unusual to say about a request it processes, you will find a strictly formatted line of data in your access log and then some warnings or errors of mostly free text nature in your error log.

The `destination` parameter takes the same values as the respective parameter of the `error_log` directive. You may still log to syslog or a file.

Modern Nginx also has an interesting performance feature of buffered access logging. You will find more information about turning buffered logging on with flush or gzip arguments at http://nginx.org/en/docs/http/ngx_http_log_module.html#access_log. Do understand what buffering means before turning it on. One of the expected features of all error reporting mechanisms is being real time and buffered logs are exactly the opposite, that is, log records are not written to disk and not made available for inspection immediately. They are held in the buffer for some time. You will need this only in high-load scenarios where writing logs starts to take noticeable time because of the disk waits.

The `log format` parameter of the `access_log` directive is the heart of access logging. It expects a name of a template that models each record in the log. You create such templates with the `log_format` directive. There is a predefined format named `combined`, which is also a good example to show here:

```
log_format combined '$remote_addr - $remote_user [$time_local] '
                    '"$request" $status $body_bytes_sent '
                    '"$http_referer" "$http_user_agent"';
```

As you can see, the `log_format` directive's second argument is a long line of variables with "talking" names. All characters between and around variables will be included in the log. Variables will be evaluated at the time of logging, and their values will take their places.

Let's look at a real example of a log record generated with this very template:

```
85.90.193.224 - - [01/Feb/2016:12:01:34 +0400] "GET / HTTP/1.0" 200
137426 "http://example.com/" "Mozilla/5.0 (Windows NT 6.1; WOW64;
rv:33.0) Gecko/20100101 Firefox/33.0"
```

You are probably very familiar with the combined log format from previous experience with Nginx, Apache, or some other web server software. Still, going through the individual items of each combined log line with us may provide you with some nonobvious insights. Let's parse the example record and learn some facts about those variables along the way:

`$remote_addr 85.90.193.224`	This is the IP address of the computer that made the request to our server. Never ever parse it as four decimal integers delimited by dots. Even the `[0-9.]+` regexp is not good enough. Can you guess the reason? Here it is:
	`2001:470:1f10:1::2 - - [28/Jan/2015:02:28:19 +0300] "HEAD / HTTP/1.1" 200...`
	We are living in the age of IPv6 in production. Big websites see 1–7% of their traffic on IPv6 (data from the end of 2015). Nginx is fully ready, so make sure your log parsers are too.

`" - - "`	The first dash is legacy. When this particular log format was born long ago and long before Nginx, there was this interesting protocol named `ident`, which allowed a host to make a connection back to the client computer and ask for the name of the user that initiated a particular TCP connection. See RFC 1413 (`https://tools.ietf.org/html/rfc1413`) if you are curious, but we should say that `ident` is long dead and not used anywhere but IRC networks. Nginx didn't even bother with implementing it; this field should be hardcoded to - always.
	The next dash is for "remote user" as identified by the HTTP auth mechanism. Which is a bit more popular than ident but not by a big margin. There is one case where HTTP auth is used relatively often, that is, closing test versions of websites from prying eyes (read: GoogleBot and other less discriminating crawlers). See the online documentation for how to configure HTTP auth at `http://nginx.org/en/docs/http/ngx_http_auth_basic_module.html`.

`"[01/Feb/2016:12:01:34 +0400]"` `$time_local`	This is the date/timestamp of the log record. Not the most convenient date/time format to parse, for sure. Be careful dealing with time zones. It still allows prefix matching, and you probably often do something along the lines of:
	`% fgrep "01/Feb/2016:12:01:" /var/log/nginx/access.log` to filter all the page hits processed during a particular minute.
	This is a more complex version that should be in your toolkit too:
	`% cat /var/log/nginx/access.log	awk '{print $4}'	awk -F : '{print $2 ":" $3}'	uniq -c`
	It will print the number of hits you had during each minute of the day. With this command, you can identify spikes that may signal a problem.
	Interestingly, the original version of this was easier:
	`% cat /var/log/nginx/access.log	awk -F : '{print $2 ":" $3}'	uniq -c` but then again, IPv6 came into our lives.
`"GET / HTTP/1.0" "$request"`	This is a string representation of the whole HTTP request. What to look for? You will be surprised by how often, along with GET and POST, you will see HEAD requests. It is a rarely discussed younger brother of GET, which is not supposed to return an actual body — only the headers of the response.
	You will not see HTTP/1.0 as a protocol very often. Modern browsers will issue HTTP/1.1 requests. All other values here should raise a flag. You will see things such as SIP/2.0 or RTSP/1.0 there; these are legitimate protocols indeed but requests for those on a website and not a SIP or RTSP endpoint are signs of scanning from malicious actors (or researchers).

`200    $status`	This is the HTTP status code. Anything besides 2xx or 3xx here indicates an error. For a comprehensive, modern, and authoritative list of HTTP status codes, please look no further than RFC 7231 (`https://tools.ietf.org/html/rfc7231`)—a rather new and long-awaited update on the HTTP/1.1 specification released in June 2014.
`137426 $body_bytes_sent`	This one does not need an explanation. We should add that it already accounts for any compression. It may also be used as a quick indicator of problems on the backend. After some time, you will learn to spot unusually small response sizes, which mean that the backend tumbled and generated a short error page instead of a normal response. Proper backends will also send a non-2xx status code but not all (and not even many) backends behave. This small Perl script searches for response sizes that are less than a tenth of the average for that URL and also less than some hard-coded chunk size threshold that is commonly used to download a part of a file: `http://kapranoff.ru/~kappa/nginx-troubleshooting/blips.pl`. We will not go over it line by line; it is just an example anyway. The idea is to make two passes of the log. First, to calculate the average bytes sent for each URI served, and second, to actually find outsiders.

`"http://example.com/" "Mozilla/5.0`
`(Windows NT 6.1; WOW64; rv:33.0)`
`Gecko/20100101 Firefox/33.0"`
`'"$http_referer" "$http_user_`
`agent"'`
	These are taken directly from HTTP request headers; they are sent by the HTTP client, usually a browser. This makes them interesting, but also non-reliable. They are, basically, strings sent to your server over the network. You cannot trust anything sent by the client. You will routinely see some fantastic user agent strings claiming to be from the future or from the past. You will also see referrer URLs that point to some totally bogus websites that do not contain any links to your site and instead try to infect you with all kinds of malware du jour.

	On the bright side, we do remember the excitement of seeing the first iPhones in our access logs during the late summer of 2007. That was fun.

There is a lot of information that you can add to your access logs using different variables that Nginx provides during processing of each request.

The whole list of them is at `http://nginx.org/en/docs/varindex.html`.

There are also several variables that are available only during log record generation and are listed in the description of the `log_format` directive at `http://nginx.org/en/docs/http/ngx_http_log_module.html#log_format`.

The recommendation is to keep saving logs in the `combined` format to be able to use a huge number of tools that community has created over the years. In addition to these, you may create some extended logs with more data to help you debug problems.

Here is a list of variables that are often useful but not included in the default `combined` format:

`$gzip_ratio`	The ratio of compressed response size to the original or `"-"` if the response was not compressed. This does not seem important, but it makes `$body_bytes_sent` more useful. Having this variable helps you to spot clients that do not support gzip compression. For them, `$body_bytes_sent` will be higher than usual.

$msec	The exact timestamp up to milliseconds. This is the same information that is available in human-readable form with $time_local, but milliseconds are important once you have a lot of hits each second.
$request_length	The size of the HTTP request. GET requests are generally short, but once they get beyond a kilobyte, you should think about having too many cookies accompanying each request. POST requests may be of any size and if your application has to accept important data from users, such as files or filled forms, you will want to monitor the size of those requests. A technique to log the contents of POST requests is described later in this chapter.
$request_time	The time between the beginning of the request and the end of the response phases. Basically, this is your atom of performance data that includes both the network and processing delays.
$sent_http_content_type	This is the content type of the response in the familiar form of something like text/html or application/pdf. It is not essential but helps when looking at logs of modern web applications and spotting that some JSON handler suddenly emitted a simple text/html response. It is also useful to calculate the total traffic divided by types of data. There is a whole family of $sent_http_* variables that correspond to the generated HTTP response headers. You may want to research what else is there. MIME types that we mention here are also discussed in *Chapter 1, Searching for Problems in Nginx Configuration*.

`$cookie_*`	The asterisk should be replaced by the name of one of your cookies. Most modern websites have some mechanism of stateful user sessions. Usually, there is a cookie named `session` or `session_id` that allows the restoration of a chain of requests that were made by one user inside one session. The remote IP address is used for that when analyzing standard combined format logs, but this may and will fail on users with the same IP or the same user hopping between IP addresses (both are absolutely normal situations).
`$host`	This one contains the hostname that processed the request. It may seem redundant because, generally, different hosts will log in to different files. However, you would be surprised to know how often logs from several hosts are processed together whether just on the same log storage cluster or even using the same log analyzer software. Having the hostname right there in the logs creates some additional freedom of not caring about filenames of the logs, and once you get tired of running greps against files and load everything into a database, you will remember the time you decided to include `$host` and thank yourself.

Logging POST requests

Once you start debugging a problem with a web application that runs behind one of your Nginx instances by tracing user requests and application responses via access logs, you will see that GET/HEAD requests are logged fully while POST request log records lack any information except the URI to which the data was posted. This is one of the questions that many system administrators ask, especially after trying to get away with `tcpdumps` only. `tcpdump` is a wonderful Swiss army knife of protocol tracing, but it requires active participation during the events that need to be traced. And tracing HTTPS with `tcpdump` is very hard.

Nginx is able to log POST request bodies and many more. You should already be fully equipped to at least try to implement such a logging yourself.

Remember that we talked about custom log formats and using variables to record the state of requests and responses. If you search through the list of variables available during request processing, you will see the variable named $request_body. See http://nginx.org/en/docs/http/ngx_http_core_module.html#var_request_body.

Let's invent a simple log format including $request_body:

```
log_format request_body_log 'body: "$request_body"';
```

Now we enable logging with this format by adding this directive:

```
access_log /var/log/nginx/requests.log request_body_log;
```

Remember that the log_format directive should be used in one of the higher contexts, for example, the http context. Multiple access_log directives may be in effect for all the requests, and because of this, we do not need to specify the rest of the variables in the template for the request_body_log format. Your usual preconfigured combined-formatted logs will still get written to.

What would we see in requests.log for some simple GET requests to download a couple of static files?

```
body: "-"
body: "-"
body: "-"
```

Make sure that you understand the result before proceeding.

Now, we need POST requests. And POST requests to static files are useless. They never happen in real life. Clients POST data to web applications, and for Nginx administrators, a web application is an upstream to which Nginx proxies the requests and from which it proxies back the responses.

Suppose that we build something like this. It will be a very simple Dancer application in Perl accepting a simple POST and responding with a piece of *dynamic HTML*.

The source code is at `http://kapranoff.ru/~kappa/nginx-troubleshooting/simple-post.pl`:

Now we will set up a proxy inside our Nginx instance:

```
location /simple-post {
    proxy_pass http://localhost:3000/;
}
```

We will point our browser to `http://localhost/simple-post`.

If the Dancer app is running, you will see a simple form of one field and a button. Type in something, click on the button and rush to your `requests.log`:

```
body: "-"
body: "a=Nginx+rules%21"
```

The first line is the empty body of the GET request for the form, whereas the second contains the body of the POST that the form generated with the help of your browser. There are two ways an HTML form may be encoded into a POST body; this one is the default **application/x-www-form-urlencoded**. The other one is **multipart/form-data;** it is widely used for forms that allow file uploads. This is a little bit out of scope of this book already. We should add that form encodings are quickly becoming a thing of the past because more and more POST bodies are constructed by the client-side JavaScript and the browsers themselves.

What is important here is that you now have a simple way to log what is coming your way via POST requests.

Conditional logging

This example will also allow demonstration of one of the more recent Nginx logging features named *conditional logging*.

The directive `access_log` has a number of optional parameters and among them is a parameter `if` that specifies a condition on which a record is appended to this particular access log. When we configured request body logging in the previous section, we still ended up with a log full of "-"; those are empty bodies of all the non-POST requests. Let's fix that. First, we add a condition to our `access_log` directive:

```
access_log /var/log/nginx/requests.log request_body_log if=$method_is_
post;
```

The condition that we use is a simple custom variable. We intentionally show this technique using syntax very similar to what is documented in the official documentation at `http://nginx.org/en/docs/http/ngx_http_log_module.html#access_log`.

So the next step for us is to create this variable. There are several ways to create a variable in Nginx. The most straightforward is using the `set` directive inside an `if` context. But it is a good habit to cringe any time you see an `if` directive in Nginx configuration. `if` should always be the last choice. Remember that there is no programming inside configuration files; everything should be as declarative as possible.

And there is a good declarative way to create a variable:

```
map $request_method $method_is_post {
    POST 1;
    default 0;
}
```

This is everything you need to do to enable conditional logging. If your Nginx version is modern enough, you will get only bodies of POST requests in your `requests.log` from now on.

There is a probability that your Nginx is not modern enough (at least 1.7.0 is required). Use `nginx -t` to test the configuration. Can you think of a way to work around the problem without upgrading Nginx? This is not a hypothetical question. Running Nginx installed from packages provided by your distribution is highly recommended, and they are notoriously not up to date.

Logging big request bodies

There is one more thing to tell you about logging request bodies. Actually, two things that will manifest in exactly the same way while having different reasons.

The variable $request_body is not guaranteed to have any content even in the case of a good POST request with data inside. The first possible reason for an empty $request_body is a situation where Nginx has decided that parsing the body is not needed and optimized it away. That is a documented behavior that still strikes in the least expected moments. The documentation says clearly:

> *"The variable's value is made available in locations processed by the proxy_pass, fastcgi_pass, uwsgi_pass, and scgi_pass directives."*

See for yourself: `http://nginx.org/en/docs/http/ngx_http_core_module. html#var_request_body`.

These are the only four cases in which Nginx populates the $request_body variable. Fortunately, POST requests to locations that do not contain any of those directives are very rare. POSTs are intended to accept data from clients and feed to server applications for which Nginx is acting as a proxy.

Be careful not to harm yourself debugging empty request bodies for some uncommon configuration with POST requests and no proxying directives in that context.

The other reason for empty $request_body is the request being too large. If the size of the request body exceeds the value set up by the `client_body_buffer_size` directive, it is not available via $request_body variable. Instead, the whole body is saved to a temporary file on the file system, and its name is written into the new $request_body_file variable.

There is also another very interesting directive named `client_body_in_file_only` that provides a way to always save requests to files. It may be used instead of the mechanism that we showed earlier altogether! You will add $request_body_file to one of your log formats and turn on `client_body_in_file_only`. After this, Nginx will create an ever-growing store of files containing all your request bodies. Do not forget to clean them up from a crontab or they will fill the filesystem.

Creating infrastructure around logs

Okay, let's do some arithmetic. Suppose that you have a rather popular but not on a world scale (yet) website with about 50,000 visits per day. This is a number that managers brag about during their meetups; they get it from some analytics software. It almost means nothing regarding your job. Because what is a visit? Let's say that what you have is an e-commerce site; you sell some nonseasonal stuff, for example, power tools. Your average visitor will look at one to two pages with spikes to early tens when actually choosing and buying something. Let it be three pages per visit on average. What is a page? For you, it is a series of HTTP responses – the main document and all the embedded objects. People notoriously underestimate the sheer size of modern web pages. It would be a safe bet to say that your pages include on average 100 objects (HTML documents, images, scripts, style sheets, and so on) amounting to the size of over a megabyte.

This will be 100 x 3 x 50,000 per day or 15,000,000 / 24 / 3600 = 174 requests per second (RPS) on average. Averaging RPS during the day will render a rather useless number unless you operate in all world's time zones and that is not very common for websites selling actual material stuff. There is a good enough heuristic to estimate peaks – multiply average by 10.

Now we have a number of lines in your daily access log (15 million) and a very rough upper limit of logging rate that you will have to deal with (a thousand and a half lines a second). These numbers all mean that you need tools because a human being is not able to consume all this information in time.

Configuring log rotation

The main and simplest tool to make the amount of logging data more manageable is log rotation. You probably have it set up already. There is a pretty standard log rotator included in many Linux distributions uninventively named `logrotate`. Its FreeBSD counterpart is `newsyslog`.

Examples of Nginx log rotation configuration in `logrotate` and `newsyslog` are shown here.

This is an example of `logrotate` configuration from a Linux box:

```
● ● ●   less nginx
/var/log/nginx/*.log {
        weekly
        missingok
        rotate 52
        compress
        delaycompress
        notifempty
        create 0640 www-data adm
        sharedscripts
        prerotate
                if [ -d /etc/logrotate.d/httpd-prerotate ]; then \
                        run-parts /etc/logrotate.d/httpd-prerotate; \
                fi \
        endscript
        postrotate
                [ -s /run/nginx.pid ] && kill -USR1 `cat /run/nginx.pid`
        endscript
}
~
~
(END)
```

And this is a sample configuration of `newsyslog` from a rather modern
FreeBSD server:

```
● ● ●   ssh kapranoff.ru
/var/log/weekly.log           640   5     1      $W6D0  JN
/var/log/wtmp                 644   3     *      @01T05 B
/var/log/xferlog              600   7     100    *      JC

/var/log/nginx-access.log     644   *     * @T00        JC /var/run/nginx.pid
/var/log/nginx-error.log      644   *     * @T00        JC /var/run/nginx.pid
~
~
~
~
~
~
~
~
~
~
~
newsyslog.conf                                          41,28
```

What they do is take care of huge logs by creating an archive of old records based on time and size of current files. It is not exactly rocket science, but there are at least several pitfalls attracting people by the numbers.

First, do have free space monitoring. And also do have monitoring of your free space monitoring. It is a surprisingly popular cause of major malfunctions. Just as the publisher warned us that the hard drive will fail while we are writing this book, because they always do, we will take the liberty of warning you that at least once in your career, disks will become totally filled up with logs. Usually, this leads to some very unpleasant effects but is easily fixable.

What are preventing measures? Set up a log store. It should be a couple of separate machines with huge and cheap (with rotating parts) mirrored disks that store your logs indefinitely. Their goal is to relieve your workhorses, actual web servers from storing log archives and from running heavy greps and messing with performance. And your rotation procedures should include copying each archive to the log store after it is created. Your processes will get a little more complex because you will have your most current log still spread out on your web servers, whereas older data will already be archived away to the log store, but it is totally worth it.

Also, move to a better compression algorithm than the default gzip. In this particular case of logs, you may save up to 50% of space just by switching from gzip. logrotate supports specifying the command it will use for compression while newsyslog has native support for both bzip2 and xz compression. xz is usually better. The only downside of using xz is high memory requirements; keep this in mind. A separate log store, again, is very useful. It may also be configured to recompress gzipped files into xz thus saving space without sacrificing performance on the web servers. The idea is to gzip the logs on the web servers, move them to the log store cluster, decompress them, and compress again with xz.

The second important part to log rotation is not losing a single record during the actual rotation. The optimal algorithm looks like this:

1. First of all, imagine that Nginx is up and running and writing log records to some `access.log` files.

2. A log rotator is fired and the `access.log` is chosen for either size or age reason.

3. The log rotator renames the `access.log` according to the rotation scheme, for example, to `access.log.0`.

4. The log rotator creates a new empty `access.log`.

5. Now, Nginx does not lose any access to the older file because it has its descriptor and the filename does not matter after the file is open by a process. So, Nginx continues to write records to `access.log.0` file.

6. The log rotator cannot compress the old file because it is still written to, so it signals Nginx to release the old file descriptor and to reopen the log file by its name again.

7. Nginx is happy to oblige. The new empty `access.log` gets opened and starts to receive new log records, whereas the old file is ready to be removed after compression.

8. The log rotator runs the compressor that creates a new file `access.log.0.xz` while deleting the old log.

It looks surprisingly complex for a seemingly simple procedure. The reason is steps 4, 5, and 6, which guarantee that logs are not renamed and deleted without Nginx knowing.

There is nothing Nginx-specific here. It just so happens that the authors thought about this problem and implemented the special `reopen` command in Nginx, which is initiated by the USR1 signal to the master process.

If your log rotator omits the command altogether, the rotation will not work at all—Nginx will always write to the old log without noticing that you renamed it. And trying to compress a file that is currently appended to is a recipe for losing some lines.

If your log rotator will restart Nginx on each rotation, then your logs will be okay, but you may lose some performance if you do graceful restarts (with the SIGHUP signal). You may even lose some requests if you do hard restarts (the old `apachectl restart` command-style restarts are not supported by Nginx executable but could be implemented with init scripts of your OS).

Working with a lot of log data

Once your Nginx installation starts to get more than several thousands of users a day, you or your managers will definitely want to get more insights from those logs. Your job will be to provide an infrastructure for that and troubleshoot problems. You can also piggyback on that endeavor to end up with a great real-time search of all your logs much more efficient than the good old grep.

The evolution of log analytics through the years is an interesting and huge topic mostly outside the scope of this book. Many of us remember the (in)famous Webalizer and AWStats packages. They are still perfectly functional, by the way, even if a bit rusty. It is not recommended to invest in these tools for modern websites though. They are not very efficient, and you will have a hard time adding the features that are expected these days.

Some of the newer solutions that are available on the market are summarized below. By all means do your own research. This is really a giant topic in itself:

- The logstash/ElasticSearch/kibana stack is a combination of Java-based tools, each of which deserves a whole book devoted to it. A working deployment allows you to store all your logs in a database indexed for all needed types of queries and reports. The kibana part of the stack provides gorgeous visualizations of time-based data. Logs are exactly that and fit perfectly. Maintaining an instance may quickly become a full-time job.

- Scribe is a central logging solution developed, open sourced, and then abandoned by Facebook. It is of historical interest only. Facebook has moved on from Scribe and if you still have a Scribe installation or have inherited one, you are in trouble. One of the easier alternatives is fluentd.

- **Fluentd** is a modern centralized logging system written in Ruby. It may be compared to the logstash part of the first stack. It has pluggable inputs and outputs. Once you have it configured to consume Nginx logs, it may feed the results to an ElasticSearch instance.

- **Apache Flume** is an older project in the family of Apache Hadoop stack of technologies. It is used to collect data into your HDFS (which is the storage for Hadoop). It is sometimes used for web logs too.

- **Splunk** is a commercial full-stack solution in order to collect, parse, store, and query logs. It calls itself "Google for your logs", and we will not comment on that. Splunk is interesting because it is also widely used to do real-time monitoring of incoming logs. A good example of such a task is intrusion detection.

Reading logs

The most interesting part for many readers ahead is that we will show you examples of different records from real Nginx log files and analyze what happened and how to fix it in each case. These will be rather simple situations many of which could be either familiar to a seasoned web system administrator or evident from the message.

We still recommend following each and every example. Sometimes, people develop a kind of selective blindness to things they do not understand fully. It is also very natural to skip unknown parts and to try to deduce their meaning from what they are surrounded with – this is how language learning works both for children and adults. Alas, human languages are highly redundant and therefore are specially catered to nonperfect, lossy understanding. Logs are usually not.

Let's start with a very simple and very famous 404 error – and how it looks from two perspectives, error log and access log.

The record from error log:

```
2016/01/29 02:25:14 [error] 18876#0: *1 "/home/kappa/books/index.
html" is not found (2: No such file or directory), client: 127.0.0.1,
server: localhost, request: "GET /books/ HTTP/1.1", host: "kantara"
```

And now the record about the same event from the access log in `combined` format:

```
127.0.0.1 - - [29/Jan/2016:02:25:14 +0300] "GET /books/ HTTP/1.1"
404 151 "-" "Mozilla/5.0 (X11; Ubuntu; Linux x86_64; rv:35.0)
Gecko/20100101 Firefox/35.0"
```

We will break them both down now.

Error log record

`"2016/01/29 02:25:14"`	This is obviously a timestamp, but note that it does not contain any time zone information. It is local time as seen by the server in its configured timezone. This minor fact means that when you transfer this log file into another timezone and do not save timezone information somewhere, your software may become confused and apply the new local timezone. After this, comparing this timestamp with the timestamp from `access_log` would be wrong.

`"[error]"`	This is the severity level of the message. Remember that earlier in this chapter we discussed the format of the `error_log` directive and there was this second parameter, the threshold. Well, this is the field that gets compared to the configured threshold to determine whether a particular message is serious enough to bother this particular system administrator with. Other possible values include things from `debug` to `emerg` (short for emergency). See the `error_log` directive documentation at `http://nginx.org/en/docs/ngx_core_module.html#error_log`.
`"18876#0:"`	Now, this part is not understood by many people. The pair of numbers gives information about which path of the Nginx ensemble of processes put this record into the log. The number before # is the PID, the identifier of the process, and the second number is the thread identifier or TID. TID is usually `0` on current Nginx on Linux. On Windows, it may be some big number. Nginx does not use multithreading in its current version. There are rumors that threads will be much more prominent on all platforms in Nginx 2.0.
`"*1"`	This is the identifier of the connection in the context of which this error happened. Actually, it is an integer counter, and it allows you to group errors by connections. By the way, the connection number and also the TID part of the previous item are not recognized by many Nginx users. Take some of your colleagues by surprise and ask about it sometime just for fun.
`"/home/kappa/books/index.html" is not found (2: No such file or directory)`	This is the actual error message formulated by Nginx accompanied by the OS-level `errno` number (`ENOENT` in this case) and `strerror` message in parentheses.
`"client: 127.0.0.1, server: localhost"`	This is the addresses of both sides of the connection. We have Nginx running right here on the workstation. This is why we see the connection over the loopback. Nginx has chosen not to do reverse DNS resolving of the client addresses for performance reasons, whereas the server name is known beforehand. This is why we see the same address in both IP and domain name forms.

`request: "GET /books/ HTTP/1.1",` `host: "kantara"`	Now, these are the data about the actual request. First, the string representation of the request itself and then the host value taken from the Host: HTTP request header sent by the browser.

It is interesting that besides the very first items in the record everything is more or less free-form and not required. The timestamp is obviously always there as are the pid and the tid (especially if it is a constant 0), but the connection is not always up and there, of course, may not be any current requests without the connection.

Error logs are notoriously not very machine-readable. You should never rely on existence of a certain type of data in a record unless you made sure that the whole record is written via a known and fixed template. For example, it is fairly easy to parse out all the ENOENT messages, but creating a summary of all types of errors will be harder.

The access log, on the contrary, is made for parsing. Let's see the record again:

```
127.0.0.1 - - [29/Jan/2016:02:25:14 +0300] "GET /books/ HTTP/1.1"
404 151 "-" "Mozilla/5.0 (X11; Ubuntu; Linux x86_64; rv:35.0)
Gecko/20100101 Firefox/35.0"
```

We already analyzed a combined record earlier in this chapter, so we won't do this again. Just look at two interesting parts.

We mentioned the weird historical date/timestamp format but at least it contains timezone and is totally unambiguous. We also see the famous 404 code in the sixth field, and that is the only sign of error here! Otherwise, it is a perfectly good HTTP request that was served with a fittingly perfect HTTP response of 151 bytes.

There will be two very popular 404 errors in your logs when you start a new website:

```
2016/02/09 19:09:11 [error] 39110#0: *1019042 open() "/site/example.
com/www/robots.txt" failed (2: No such file or directory), client:
157.55.39.200, server: example.com, request: "GET /robots.txt
HTTP/1.1", host: "example.com"
2010/10/17 22:44:05 [error] 44858#0: *809 open() "/site/example.
com/favicon.ico" failed (2: No such file or directory), client:
95.26.237.86, server: example.com, request: "GET /favicon.ico
HTTP/1.1", host: "example.com"
```

These are the so-called *well-known* files that HTTP clients request and use. You should get some `robots.txt` and some favicon for your sites at least for the sake of your own sanity. Refer to `http://www.robotstxt.org/` and `https://en.wikipedia.org/wiki/Favicon` for more information on these files.

It is time to see some more errors:

```
2016/02/09 13:19:00 [error] 39110#0: *1014628 kevent() reported
that connect() failed (61: Connection refused) while connecting to
upstream, client: 204.8.105.53, server: example.com, request: "GET /
admin.php HTTP/1.0", upstream: "http://127.0.0.1:3000/admin.php",
host: "example.com"
```

You should read this almost effortlessly. This is an example of Nginx acting as a proxy, and this is certainly the most popular use for it. Being a proxy, this Nginx instance is trying to connect to an upstream on behalf of a client. The upstream that has problems is listed in the end before the familiar host item. The mentioned kevent() is the so-called *implementation detail* that should not have leaked here but well, it has. It is a part of the mechanism Nginx uses to work with network connections under FreeBSD, Mac OS X, and other BSD operating systems.

On a Linux box, the same record would look like this:

```
2014/07/29 10:18:41 [error] 14243#0: *100053182 connect() failed
(111: Connection refused) while connecting to upstream, client:
37.73.249.120, server: example.com, request: "GET /example.com/404
HTTP/1.1", upstream: "http://[2c32:6d8:0:172a::318]:8080/", host:
"example.com"
```

What is interesting in that record? First, no kevent(). Second, the errno code has changed! And indeed, our FreeBSD and Linux boxes have 61 and 111 for ECONNREFUSED, respectively. So no, you cannot rely on this code and more so you cannot rely on the Connection refused string. On Windows the same error may have this message: **10060: A connection attempt failed because the connected party did not properly respond after a period of time, or established connection failed because connected host has failed to respond.**

And second, the upstream is using IPv6, which may break some scripts if they search for the TCP port number after the first colon.

We want to show you another special kind of **file not found** errors that are a sign of modern times:

```
2016/01/24 18:28:09 [error] 39111#0: *755667 open() "/site/example.
com/www/wp-login.php" failed (2: No such file or directory), client:
109.198.238.60, server: example.com, request: "GET /wp-login.php
HTTP/1.1", host: "www.example.com"
2016/01/24 18:27:01 [error] 39111#0: *755651 open() "/site/example.
com/www/administrator/index.php" failed (2: No such file or
directory), client: 82.199.126.95, server: example.com, request: "GET
/administrator/index.php HTTP/1.1", host: "example.com"
```

These are only interesting because they come from bots that attempt to hack into your system. They are very persistent in trying some URLs that look like administration or login scripts and that never ever existed on your site.

It is too cheap for them to just try any host they see on the Internet without even having a database of unsuccessful attempts. They will come from thousands of different IP addresses many of which will look totally innocent because those are infected computers all over the world controlled centrally. They have become a norm already; you should not most of the time even bother with any countermeasures (unless of course you run some old installation of WordPress, and in this case, you are probably hacked already and earn money for these people by serving some porn ads to your users alongside your own content).

Here is an error that contains much less information:

```
2014/07/29 00:00:18 [info] 14238#0: *95951600 client 77.205.98.18
closed keepalive connection
```

Can you guess why? Because, as we said a little bit earlier, errors happen all the time even when there is no request under processing. This is exactly the case: a client closed a connection that was left open after a successful request/response pair as a way to optimize the following requests. This is named KeepAlive. Nginx is happy to serve many requests in one connection consequently, but the client is free to close the connection at any time. Now you should understand why this information has [info] instead of [error]. Ideas about whether you should do anything about it are left as an exercise.

```
2014/07/29 00:02:11 [info] 14241#0: *95959742 client timed out (110:
Connection timed out) while waiting for request, client: 62.90.94.31,
server: 0.0.0.0:443
```

A similar message not having any information about a request because it is actually an error of not being able to get the request before timeout.

```
2014/07/29 00:00:18 [info] 14238#0: *95951764 SSL_read() failed
(SSL: error:14094412:SSL routines:SSL3_READ_BYTES:sslv3 alert bad
certificate:SSL alert number 42) while waiting for request, client:
176.115.120.138, server: 0.0.0.0:443
```

It is quite an enigmatic error message that you won't be able to do anything about. The SSL code is complex, and there are a lot of weird SSL implementations out there. Something went wrong. You should take note and either try to reproduce or wait for more of the same.

```
2014/07/29 00:02:24 [info] 14240#0: *95968051 client sent too long
URI while reading client request line, client: 87.244.170.11, server:
example.com, request: "GET /log_error?login=takoe&error=<some very-
very long string>
```

We trimmed this one by hand because it took almost the whole screen. There is a limit on the total size of the request headers. It may be changed with the `large_client_header_buffers` directive. See `http://nginx.org/en/docs/http/ngx_http_core_module.html#large_client_header_buffers` for more information. This is definitely something that you may fix by increasing the configured value, but we would recommend against it and speak to your application developers team instead. It looks like they have chosen the wrong tool for their task here. Requests of such size should use the POST method instead of GET.

There is another error we wanted to show here as an example of what problems really big websites face sometimes:

```
2013/05/16 12:21:11 [crit] 21947#0: *31843937 open() "/usr/local/
nginx/html/50x.html" failed (24: Too many open files), client:
88.2.3.44, server: example.com, request: "GET /file/images/background.
jpg HTTP/1.1", upstream: "http://10.10.4.1:81//file/images/background.
jpg", host: "example.com"
```

You should be able to read and understand every single character of that message now. What exactly is **24: Too many open files**? There is a limit on the number of files that any single process can hold open. Usually, the limit is really big. Run this command to see the limit your shell has:

```
% ulimit -Sn
```

Once you have your Nginx serving more files than that simultaneously, this error will appear in the error log. Nginx has a way of increasing the limit itself, see `http://nginx.org/en/docs/ngx_core_module.html#worker_rlimit_nofile`. Increasing the hard limits for all processes is OS-dependent. On Linux, you will need to add something like `fs.file-max = 50000` to your `/etc/sysctl.conf` and then run the following code:

```
% sysctl -p
```

Downloading the example code

You can download the example code files for this book from your account at http://www.packtpub.com. If you purchased this book elsewhere, you can visit http://www.packtpub.com/support and register to have the files e-mailed directly to you.

You can download the code files by following these steps:

1. Log in or register to our website using your e-mail address and password.
2. Hover the mouse pointer on the **SUPPORT** tab at the top.
3. Click on **Code Downloads & Errata**.
4. Enter the name of the book in the **Search** box.
5. Select the book for which you're looking to download the code files.
6. Choose from the drop-down menu where you purchased this book from.
7. Click on **Code Download**.

Once the file is downloaded, please make sure that you unzip or extract the folder using the latest version of:

- WinRAR/7-Zip for Windows
- Zipeg/iZip/UnRarX for Mac
- 7-Zip/PeaZip for Linux

Summary

In this chapter, we refreshed our knowledge of how logging works in Nginx. There are two types of logs; one of them may be infinitely extended, whereas the other is hard to parse by scripts because it does not have enough structure.

We spent some time on special topics, such as log rotation and logging POST request bodies (with a small test stand that we created step by step in the chapter, no less).

We also analyzed several error records from some real error logs.

The next chapter will have more actual problems analyzed and troubleshot. We will present several cases of actual problems that people had with read Nginx installations and try to debug them from the ground up.

3
Troubleshooting Functionality

You get a call in the middle of the night. "Our website isn't working," your boss yells. In seconds, you are wide awake and trying to remember "what exactly did we change yesterday?" — this is a very natural reaction for every system administrator on this planet.

Have you ever been in such a situation? This is a stress test for each young sysadmin, and we hope you have had this earlier in your career rather than later because it is a teaching experience. Fortunately, websites usually malfunction when they are mostly loaded and this happens during the late morning or early evening hours — if you are lucky to live in roughly the same time zone as your target audience. For example, this is a traffic graph for a big website in Russia, which is a country very centered around its two capitals, and those cities are both in UTC+03 time zone as of 2016:

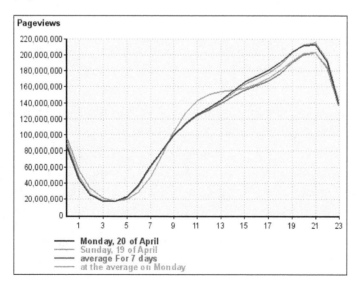

As you can see, the real traffic comes in the morning, has a peak in the evening, and falls sharply as people go to bed.

This chapter will cover the following topics:

- A process to use when working on such an incident, far from perfect but very workable
- A description of some of the most shameful failures
- A brief section on how to restart Nginx
- More information about some ways you may save the day with Nginx

Processing a complain

Let us call any expressed case of unexpected behavior a complain. The term is vague enough not to imply that it is always a problem or an error, which was introduced during development and needs to be fixed. Working on a complain starts with investigation. The only thing that you know from the beginning is that something on your website does not work for someone. The incidents raised as a result of automatic monitoring systems are a separate case.

Surprisingly, people in general are rarely capable of answering the question of "What exactly does not work for you?" Some of them get confused or even angry. While you must always ask this, do not get high hopes. Let us analyze some of the possible answers from the most popular to less so:

- *"Nothing!"*
- *"I load the page, I click there and there, order a book, get to my shopping cart, initiate payment, get confirmation and on the last step there a security warning about some sort of certificate which expired yesterday"*

Most of the time, the burden of determining how exactly the problem manifests itself is on you. You need to get your priorities right and act quickly.

This chapter presents you with a series of steps to perform when all you have is a report of your website not working. The list is not flat; there are branches here and there, which you must follow. At the same time, we recommend reading all the steps as this will help you grasp the general procedure better. You may also use the steps during an incident. In that case, you will start at the very beginning and then choose the appropriate next step while skipping the irrelevant. For many of the readers, a description of this format as similar to a very simple finite-state machine may be helpful.

You will move from one state to another by interpreting additional signals and hope to arrive to the finish. This is a three-level scheme of a simple troubleshooting process that we prefer. Each of the boxes will be explained later:

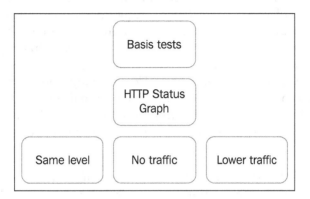

Rolling back

We need to provide a very important sidenote here. A step zero, if you want, is always trying to bring the system into a working state by removing recent changes. Websites are software that is infinitely more dynamic than anything we had before. If you deploy weekly, you are actually slower than many of your competitors. So when something happens, the probability of a recent set of changes being the culprit is very high.

It is very important to always hold dearly to the main goal of all your actions during such an event; you are searching for a workaround that will allow the business to go on. You need to bring the operations back as soon as possible and only after that you should start searching for the root cause and inventing a strategy of dealing with it once and for all. One of the great sins of young system administrators, especially with developer background, is *premature debugging*, which I define as spending resources (even if it is just your mental resources and not company money) on the fix without first implementing a quick and dirty workaround.

One of the easiest ways to work around a new problem is to roll back your software to a previous, working version. Organizations that have a good discipline of change control may even choose to roll back on any failure whether it is caused internally or externally. The hardest part is usually on the application server side of things and you, as being responsible for the stability of the service, may require your development team to implement comprehensive rolling back capabilities. There are several things that you may do yourself on the Nginx level though.

Keeping Nginx configuration under source control

Nginx configuration files are all plain text written in a simple line and block-oriented language. This combination is as perfect for diffing and merging as any "real source code document." So please, do invest into setting up a source code repository for your Nginx configuration. It absolutely does not matter if you choose the good old *Subversion* or the modern workhorse *Git* or even the squeaky in the joints but still functional *CVS*. Any of those will save your sanity many times in comparison with a system without any source control system. The next step from having just a central repo is automating the whole deployment. That bit is a little out of the scope of this book, but inquisitive readers should definitely get interested in modern automation tools, such as *Chef*, *RX* or *Ansible*, once they have more than five servers in their zone of responsibility.

Having access to all the previous versions of your config files alone is a wonderful thing that will greatly ease the rolling back process. Any sane source control system allows you to tag specific revisions, to check out based on timestamp or to create moving branches. A very quick way to enhance a working server with this source control magic is a tool named **etckeeper** (see `https://github.com/joeyh/etckeeper`). It will automatically record all the changes you make to `/etc` and therefore allow you to jump to the past in case of trouble. It will also regularly mail the diffs to the administrator of the server. It may seem a little bit too automatic for a server, but it is a good start.

This is a simple command that you may issue in an etckeeper-controlled `/etc` folder to quickly revert some changes in `/etc/nginx`:

```
% sudo git checkout 'master@{11 minute ago}' nginx
```

Keeping a case journal

A highly recommended piece of best practice when investigating a website malfunction is to keep a log or journal of ideas to implement afterwards. This will leave you with a list of things to require from yourself and your colleagues in the development and management departments to prevent any new cases of this particular problem. This is why we will mark each step with things to write down into such a journal. You should dump any crazy or trivial ideas into this journal so that you could free your mind for the urgent task at hand. Even if you reject most of the ideas afterwards, keeping this journal will help you during the process.

So, without further ado, let's start.

Again, what we have is a just vague complaint about a website you are responsible for. Someone said that it was not working.

Performing the simplest test

Load the page yourself. This is not the most effective step, but you will do that anyway, won't you? It is a natural reflex — the important part is not to come to any premature conclusions. If it does not load, you should start with checking your internet connection. See the later text.

If the page works for you, you will feel a false relief. Actually, your problem potentially just got harder. The website works for some people (in this case, it works for you) but may not work for everyone. See the *HTTP response traffic* section here.

By the way, you may sometimes have the answer right here. For example, you will immediately see expired SSL certificates. See also *Certificate test*.

Performing the Internet connection test

Check that your own internet connection is okay by trying to load a reference web page, for example, `https://www.google.com`.

Why is this a separate test at all? Shouldn't we also talk about electricity or clean air then? Two reasons: if you are a small company in a rented office space even in the most advanced countries of the world, chances are that you will get two–three incidents of ISP failure a year. Also, we need a smooth transition to talk about backup connection kits for sysadmins.

> Journal: Have a permanent indication of your own connection to the Internet working. Curiously, many people use the Dropbox icon in the tray for that. While this is a cute lifehack, please implement something more professional, office-wide and/or for your workstation.

You need to have a backup Internet connection for the rare case of your main connection failure. Nowadays, it is usually a mobile phone with a tethering setup. Fire it up and redo the tests. It is surprisingly unpopular to have a backup connection ready, and we would like to say a few words about it. Traditionally, backups are storage. Your office administrators will mirror the disks; you yourself have a loyal trusted Time Machine setup at home for your kids' photographs and documents. But in this day and age, with all applications moved or moving to the cloud, storage backup systems lose their importance. You won't built anything remotely comparable with what Dropbox has (with the help of Amazon Web Services) yourself. Scale effects buy additional redundancy and talent. But at the same time, the importance of your connection rises.

A modern Chromebook is a fast and cheap workhorse machine right until the WiFi vanishes because the access point power supply brick got scorched or something. Modern IT people feel less pressure with the storage backup and should use the freed resources to ensure connection backups instead. Think about your options and invest in an alternative way to bring back your office online maybe even with less bandwidth. You will be happy when this system helps you. And think of it exactly as you did about your storage backups; these are risk aversion systems. They are not required to ever be used, not even once to still be considered a successful investment.

Journal: 1) Implement backup uplink for your office. 2) Equip all your system administrators (for example, yourself) with remote administration kits. The recommended way is to provide them with separate devices (either wireless 3G/LTE dongles or smartphones with preconfigured tethering) and prepaid data plans. Do not rely on their main phones because those tend to have problems with charge and traffic during the most important moments, whereas a separate company-provided device may be required to be fully charged by rules when the person is on duty.

Testing the general HTTP response traffic

Look at your general HTTP monitoring graph or at least `tail -f` the access log. This is the most informative way of knowing what the effects of the incident are, if they exist. You have to have the infrastructure in place, and we will explain a way of establishing one in *Chapter 6, Monitoring Nginx*. The general HTTP graph will contain a chart of how many HTTP response codes your site generated each minute. You are most interested in the level of 200 responses. There are several possibilities, as follows:

- The number of 200 responses dropped to zero or you cannot reach your monitoring.

- The number of 200 responses dropped to a lower level but above zero. Both of these indicate ongoing damage to business with a high level of probability. We will discuss them properly later (see the *No traffic* and *Lower traffic* cases) right after we deal with the more easy case.

- You have roughly the same level of 200 responses as you do usually at this time this day of the week.

This is a good place to be. Your website is likely serving your visitors in the same way it did. This is the time when you have to involve people from development because right now, these are the ways that the website may still not do what is expected.

Journal: Implement this type of general HTTP monitoring—an area chart of four colors for 200, 3xx, 4xx, and 5xx HTTP responses as per the Nginx access logs with 1-minute granularity and a number of alert thresholds.

Detecting a lying application

The application behind Nginx does not actually work but still generates responses with HTTP 200 Ok code. This is a major crime.

Good websites never show internal error messages to users. There is no need to scare people with unnecessary details, and this would never even be discussed if sometimes websites would not go too far by hiding HTTP response codes too. There is nothing to stop anyone from responding with 200 Ok in all cases and indicating error condition only in the content part of the response. This way is "machine-unreadable" for many practical purposes. All the bots and crawlers will not consider such an error to be an error. Your monitoring software will also need special processing to distinguish these cases.

See examples for the famous **404 Not Found** error:

```
% curl -sLI http://google.com/non-existent | fgrep HTTP/
HTTP/1.1 301 Moved Permanently
HTTP/1.1 404 Not Found

% curl -sLI http://live.com/non-existent | fgrep HTTP/
HTTP/1.1 301 Moved Permanently
HTTP/1.1 301 Moved Permanently
HTTP/1.1 302 Found
HTTP/1.1 200 OK
```

Unfortunately, this situation means that you still have not found the problem, you only have found that you lack an easy way to find it.

 Journal: Create issues in your bug tracker for all cases of not reporting errors with an HTTP response code. Developers should fix those.

The developers should be working shoulder to shoulder with you now. Although they are scouting the inner workings of their application code, which is happily generating error messages by the numbers without a single 4xx/5xx HTTP response code, you could provide some help by searching for the URLs that started to emit a wildly different amount of traffic. Do you remember the script that we wrote together in the Logging Chapter? If you have response size in your logs, with some modifications, it will find lines that contain a number too far away from the average.

 Journal: The top class of monitoring systems applies the theory of disorder detection.

There are ways to automatically trigger events on sudden unexpected changes in a random process (and a stream of numbers that you monitor is such a process). Another keyword for you to search for is "anomaly detection." All the systems that we have met were proprietary, developed in-house to the needs of very large Internet companies. There are some commercial offerings in this space, for example, Splunk. You might actually have a go at this type of monitoring without returning to school for another degree by monitoring the first derivative of the 200 HTTP response number and triggering events on a level of the derivative that is beyond a certain threshold. Because the first derivative is an indicator of change, high values will correspond to sharp spikes up or down.

Working around an integration failure

Your website implements part of its functionality by transparently integrating another service, which is having an incident.

This is a situation when someone else entirely is at fault. Examples of such configuration include using external commenting systems, advertisement placement systems, statistics and/or tracking software. Your job here is to try switching off unessential external components. Because this will require removing pieces of application code (even if it is a simple HTML block in a number of static pages), we cannot provide you with any specific details. You also should thoroughly document which services are blocking your operation.

 Journal: 1) Implement monitoring of external services. 2) Invent a plan of graceful degradation and implement it. 3) Require asynchronous client-side inclusions.

Graceful degradation is an interesting concept of having a special mode of operation for the times when an unessential part of your website (external or not) does not work. For many businesses going into full read-only mode may be graceful enough. Not being able to place an order is certainly much more desirable for an electronic bookstore than not responding at all and thus losing credibility in the eyes of all search engines, which will happily ditch your sites from their search results immediately.

Planning for graceful degradation should start early in the design process. That is a topic for a whole separate book or two, of course. At these stages, you should at the very least regularly annoy development about it and do as much as possible yourself.

Some other examples of degradation that may be implemented as extreme measures to live through some rough periods are:

- Removing a full-text search functionality for a while. This is usually a CPU-intensive and disk-intensive operation used by a single-digit percentage of your visitors.
- Hiding social functions such as commenting and sharing.

Shouldn't we strive to build a system that does not need chopping one of its legs off from time to time? Of course we should. But costs may be prohibitively high. You cannot plan to work flawlessly under **Distributed Denial of Service** attack from a malicious competitor if you are a start-up. This would just cost you too much.

Nginx has several tricks up its sleeve to work around external failures.

The try_files directive

This directive provides a way to quickly serve a local file instead of performing an upstream request. It is important enough to be presented here. The general format is:

```
try_files file1 file2 … uri;
```

Almost always, `try_files` is used inside a location block that forms a context specifying which requests should be processed from local files. The idea may be illustrated by this example:

```
location /get-recommendations {
  try_files static-recs.html empty.html @recommender_engine;
}
location @recommender_engine {
  proxy_pass http://ml-fuzzy-bigdata-pipeline/compute-personal-
  recommendations?for=$user;
}
```

What we have here is a separate system that uses some buzzword-compliant recommendation generation technology to provide your website visitors with some personalized product offers. These tend to be fragile, and `try_files` protects us by specifying a fallback static HTML file. The order of processing might confuse some people. First, the static files are tried from left to right. Once an existing file is found, it is used to form the response and the remaining files and named URI block are not used.

Normally, those static files do not exist on the filesystem at all. They get created by the monitoring system (or people) in case of emergency. After you or your colleagues carefully raise the heavy external component from the dead, you remove the static file and Nginx starts to issue actual queries to the upstream.

Setting up automatic removal from upstream

Another mechanism provided by Nginx that may help you in these situations is the glorious upstream module. This is a whole subsystem that augments the venerable `proxy_pass` directive with a lot of failover options. The idea is that instead of good old URLs pointing to external sources of data to use to generate responses for client requests, you point to a composite object configured via `upstream` block directive. This block is useful together with its contents only, so let me start with an example:

```
upstream ml-backend {
    server machine-learning1.example.com;
    server machine-learning2.example.com;
    server unix:/var/run/mld.sock backup;
}
```

And then later on:

```
location @recommender_engine {
    proxy_pass http://ml-backend/compute;
}
```

Upstreams defined with the `upstream` directives may be used in all the following five client (request-making) modules of Nginx: `proxy`, `fastcgi`, `uwsgi`, `scgi`, and `memcached`. They all share similar-looking directives to set up external resources to use while serving requests from actual clients. The main directive is always `*_pass`, and it is exactly what we use for the example.

What this block does is combine a group of servers into an object with some embedded group behavior. First, there is rotation. When a `*_pass` directive is used to process a request by passing to such an upstream object, the actual server is chosen from all the configured alternatives.

The algorithm to choose the server is not random. The servers are sequenced in a round-robin fashion. You may also provide relative weights of each server inside one group. For simplicity, it is convenient to think that the choice is random. In the long run, the probability of each variant for weighted round robin will be roughly equal to the corresponding probability of the same variant for the weighted random distribution.

The interesting bit of logic that upstream contains is removing failed servers from the pool of available choices. This logic is controlled by a number of parameters:

`max_fails=$number`	This is a number of failed attempts needed for this particular server to become "failed" and be removed from rotation. These failures must happen during a fixed period of time specified in the next parameter.
`fail_timeout=$duration`	This variable is used for two distinct purposes. First, it specifies the length of the period to count failed attempts. Second, it is also used actively as a time for which the failed server stays failed without reconsideration. One might have some problems with reusing the same value, but things are how they are.
`backup`	This is a binary or Boolean parameter. When it exists, the marked server is only chosen when all the other, non-backup servers are marked as failed.

You probably already know the way to use the described upstream functionality to implement failover for external services that you invoke on the server side. The example on the previous page demonstrates exactly that. The named location `@recommender_engine` is an HTTP proxy tunneling the requests to a group of three servers, two of which look very similar and probably are just copies of each other for the sake of balancing. The third one is a local server listening on a UNIX domain socket. This might be a simpler application not providing any actual recommendation and not having any buzzwords inside, just serving some static data. You might even proxy to the very same instance of Nginx you are writing the configuration file for!

Configuring the good old SSI

Server-Side Includes (**SSI**) is an old technology of very simple dynamic generation of HTTP responses totally inside the web server software, Nginx in your case. Nginx SSI is a descendant of the old Apache SSI with some useful features. SSI syntax and the mode of operation are well documented at `http://nginx.org/en/docs/http/ngx_http_ssi_module.html`. In short, it is a way to paste pieces of data into your HTTP responses from inside Nginx in a fast, efficient, and controllable manner. You may use it instead of implementing this functionality in your application code with some HTTP client library. Nginx will asynchronously fetch a URL with all the proper timeouts and gracefully fail to a default block if the remote side is slow or dead.

Asynchronous inclusion is a pretty standard modern way of embedding active resources (read: scripts) in a web page in a way that allows browser to never block waiting for these scripts to be fetched and executed. It is a job of a frontend engineer to make sure that anything included is working asynchronously. You may be of help by providing "annoyance" and also a testing stand where the entire Internet is blackholed except your site. By the word blackholing here, I mean a specific method of dropping packets in the firewall that will make connections not be refused but hang and wait for timeout on the client side.

There were several incidents when a popular Internet counter failure slowed down a significant number of independent websites. There is no excuse to include counters synchronously.

Both the cases of a *Lying application* and *Integration failure* will also eventually lead to lower levels of 200 responses because people will stop using a website that technically works but does not serve their needs.

 Journal: Implement proper escalation procedures. At all times, you should know whom to call if one of the hosts mentioned in one of your upstream blocks inside the Nginx configuration is misbehaving.

Planning for more complete monitoring

Many big modern websites consist of not only hundreds of hosts but hundreds of clusters of hosts. Each of those clusters performs a specific role in the whole grand scheme of things, whereas individual servers serve the requests providing load balancing and high availability. The role of the entry point to such a cluster is often delegated to a couple of Nginx boxes with a hardware-based load balancer in front of them.

Each of those may fail. To work around a part of your own externally facing infrastructure failure, you first find it by looking manually at a waterfall of the page load provided by a modern browser and then either switching the blocking part off or quickly fixing it.

 Journal: Establish a process where you never open a group of web servers to the outside without having a general HTTP monitoring of the type described above for those particular servers. Also, consider all unmonitored servers as "critical" bugs requiring fixing right after all the "blocking" problems go away and before anything else.

Processing a situation of no traffic

You probably don't serve your users at all. This is the worst scenario for your business. All your efforts should be *not* on fixing the problem but on working around it. You will debug and fix the problem the right way later, but now you need to throw everything at bringing the service back up.

One very useful practice in such a situation is to put one of the malfunctioning servers *on ice*, that is, removing it from production but leaving it alone for the sake of preserving the erroneous state intact. A full disk, a busy waiting process hogging the CPU—let the machine keep doing that until you have enough time for actual thorough debugging. It is only natural to try cleaning up right away, but you may destroy the vital evidence by removing a single core dump or a seemingly archived log. We know that it would be hard to be vaguer than that, but the specifics require knowing your exact configuration and the details of the trouble you are facing. Sometimes, it is enough to remove an IP address from an upstream block in `nginx.conf`.

Returning to our example with a heavy backend machine-learning cluster:

```
upstream ml-backend {
    server machine-learning1.example.com;
    server machine-learning2.example.com;
    server unix:/var/run/mld.sock backup;
}
```

Removing `machine-learning1` from the block and leaving it alone will make further investigations possible after you bring the second host up and start serving users.

First, you check the connectivity to the actual Nginx servers. You run a `ping` command, leave it in the background for a minute to see the packet loss, and immediately try connecting to the 80 port via a Telnet program. If you see `ping` bailing out with:

```
ping: unknown host
```

... you have likely found the problem.

Your domain expired. This is the most stupid problem to have. People get fired for that. But this still happens a lot which is insane. One of the popular scenarios for smaller shops is when the owner of the business wants to keep ultimate control of the property in their own hands and keeps the credentials to the domain registrar to themselves but does not have time and resources to actually react to all those renewal reminder e-mails. This sounds unprofessional, but it happens frequently.

Currently, you have to demand those credentials or demand that they log in and immediately pay the registrar to keep the domains delegated.

 Journal: Have separate monitoring for all the domains your business uses. There are online tools that will check the expiration regularly; you will find them in abundance. There are also plugins for popular monitoring packages such as Nagios.

```
kappa@kantara: ~
kantara:~[2]%                                                    13:38
kantara:~[2]% ping machine-learning1.example.com                 13:38
ping: unknown host machine-learning1.example.com
kantara:~[2]%                                                    13:38
```

Other bad signs are: `ping` is hanging, and packet loss is way above zero. This is the time you call your hosting provider support while simultaneously trying to ping from another location. You should have a server or two in a completely different data center from your main operation, so you just `ssh` to one of them and ping your website from there.

This is a case of some severe packet loss happening between me and Twitter's `t.co` service. Most of the time, it is a sign of problems on your side, not theirs. But rare things happen, and you should be ready for that:

```
kappa@kantara: ~
kantara:~[0]% ping t.co                                          13:47
PING t.co (199.16.156.11) 56(84) bytes of data.
64 bytes from 199.16.156.11: icmp_seq=1 ttl=246 time=151 ms
64 bytes from 199.16.156.11: icmp_seq=3 ttl=246 time=151 ms
64 bytes from 199.16.156.11: icmp_seq=6 ttl=246 time=151 ms
64 bytes from 199.16.156.11: icmp_seq=9 ttl=246 time=151 ms
64 bytes from 199.16.156.11: icmp_seq=11 ttl=246 time=151 ms
64 bytes from 199.16.156.11: icmp_seq=14 ttl=246 time=151 ms
64 bytes from 199.16.156.11: icmp_seq=16 ttl=246 time=151 ms
64 bytes from 199.16.156.11: icmp_seq=17 ttl=246 time=151 ms
64 bytes from 199.16.156.11: icmp_seq=19 ttl=246 time=151 ms
64 bytes from 199.16.156.11: icmp_seq=20 ttl=246 time=151 ms
64 bytes from 199.16.156.11: icmp_seq=22 ttl=246 time=151 ms
64 bytes from 199.16.156.11: icmp_seq=23 ttl=246 time=151 ms
64 bytes from 199.16.156.11: icmp_seq=24 ttl=246 time=151 ms
64 bytes from 199.16.156.11: icmp_seq=25 ttl=246 time=151 ms
^C
--- t.co ping statistics ---
26 packets transmitted, 14 received, 46% packet loss, time 34237ms
rtt min/avg/max/mdev = 151.303/151.410/151.521/0.363 ms
kantara:~[0]%                                                    13:48
kantara:~[0]%                                                    13:48
```

If `ping` cannot reach your server from there either, start rebooting your servers.

You should have a way to reboot an otherwise unreachable server; every modern hosting provider has it, whether in the form of a simple menu item **Reboot**, such as in Amazon EC2 or a whole **Intelligent Platform Management Interface (IPMI)** console access.

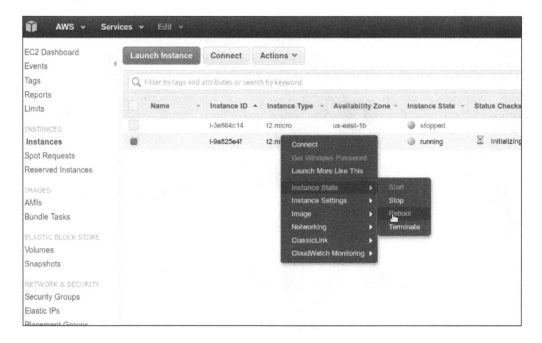

Reboot helps surprisingly often. It may also destroy evidence (for example, if you have a "run-away" process hung on a rare bug that will be killed on reboot), but being online is still more valuable.

If you cannot reboot or it didn't help, you should be talking to your hosting provider already. They may have some kind of connectivity trouble. Otherwise, you might be a victim of DDoS, and your hoster has already initiated its anti-DDoS measures.

Journal: Make sure that you have a quick way to reboot any of your servers remotely. Gone are the days when such a request required an engineer to go looking for your hardware in the racks. What is important is having the startup sequences right. Usually, Nginx boxes are stateless (or have only discardable state like cache) and come back themselves, but please test them often. It is sometimes too easy to make a live configuration change without saving it.

You haven't yet found your problem if the server is reachable and your `telnet` to the `80` port shows the following output:

Nginx is working, but because it is your application that is usually behind Nginx that carries the logic of the business, your website is useless. This is where you switch hats; now you need to bring up the upstream.

There are several ways in which Nginx connects to the upstream application. It may be a rather simple HTTP proxy. This is what historically is called the "reverse proxy" or "web accelerator" mode. It may also use FastCGI or other technology stack-specific protocols, such as WSGI or PSGI.

The HTTP mode is easier to debug, and you should recommend it to your developers although in the end it is their decision which interface to use. Nginx equally supports all of them.

Finding a problem in your application code is also beyond the scope of our book. You may have a database failure or an actual software bug. What you may do now, besides engaging developers, is provide your visitors with a nice humble static page explaining that you have temporary technical problems. A simple way to redirect all requests to a single location is this:

```
server {
    redirect http://somewhere.on.s3.example.com/status.html 302;
}
```

This will return a specially crafted HTTP response to all requests. The response will have `302` status code (which is the closest to "temporary redirect") and a Location: header with the value you provide.

If telnet gives you

```
telnet: Unable to connect to remote host: Connection refused
```

or hangs on the phase "Trying 392.1.2.3..." then read on.

Journal:

1) Make sure that you have a way to check connectivity from an external location. 2) Probably move to another hosting provider. 3) Plan a meeting about having a failover scenario for network failure; yes, you can spread out to another data center, but this is a very interesting topic reaching way beyond of the scope of this book.

We are now on one of those steps where hopes are high. Nginx rarely crashes, but no response on the `80` port may be a sign of a crash. Try logging in to the server with `ssh`. If you fail for whatever reason, reboot your servers and start from there. See information about rebooting the earlier.

Once you are done with it, immediately restart Nginx. The exact commands will depend on the type of OS you use.

On FreeBSD, this is as simple as the following:

```
% sudo /usr/local/etc/rc.d/nginx restart
```

On Debian-based Linux distributions, it is either:

```
% sudo service nginx restart
```

...for Debian 8.0 and higher or:

```
% sudo /etc/init.d/nginx restart
```

Restarting a daemon serving network requests is an important operation. Although this particular failure usually means that it does not serve anything right now, we would like to use the occasion to describe how Nginx authors solved the problem of restarts.

Restarting Nginx properly

There are several modes of restart operation that Nginx implements and the administrator is able to control which method is used by sending different signals to the Nginx master process. Remember that you send signals with the `kill` command. Nginx operates as a flock of processes, and the ones that are processing the requests are the worker processes. We will delve deeper into this in the next chapter. You almost never need to signal the worker processes. Instead, you send signals to the master process, which in turn organizes the shutdown and restart of all the worker processes.

These are the signals that initiate different restart modes:

Signal	Mode
HUP	This is the hangup signal. After receiving this signal, Nginx will perform the so-called graceful restart, that is, it will restart without any downtime. There won't be a single HTTP request that went unserved or interrupted. The idea behind this mode is to start new worker processes for new requests while waiting for the old workers to finish processing of older requests and then remove them.
USR2	This custom user signal allows you to completely change the binary of Nginx. This means full restart including even the master processes. There would be a moment when two masters are running with one of them "handing the job over" to the other. This mode is needed when you built a newer Nginx with some patches.

After a restart, you may have two basic outcomes. First, you see that Nginx has successfully restarted. Check that connections to the port 80 can be opened. You may have just fixed the problem. If not, your Nginx may have crashed again. Your next steps involve the careful reading of the error logs of Nginx itself and also system logs of the operating system (usually, `/var/log/messages`). This is probably the most unpleasant moment in the whole investigation process. We have to leave this entirely to you unfortunately. We are in the realm of debugging a crash of a very stable piece of software, which means that you have some very unusual, unexpected situation that requires a custom solution. See the *Chapter 2, Logging in to Nginx* for more insights.

Do you remember rolling back? Try to roll back the entire configuration of the server. Try downgrading software and kernel.

Journal: Implement high-availability measures on the level before Nginx. This is a step deeper into network configuration, but you will need this sooner or later. Read about CARP, Cisco IP balancing or maybe switch to a cloud provider such as Amazon and use their own solutions. You need a way to switch a misbehaving Nginx instance off while replacing it with a working clone on the same IP address.

Second, you may see an error message about a problem during the start process. If Nginx does not start, it will always report the reason for that—be it a simple error in configuration files or something more serious. This happens very often, which is surprising. An overconfident young sysadmin makes a change to `nginx.conf` and then neither commits it to a VCS, nor even restarts Nginx. After a while when you need to make a restart, you see this screenful of terror:

```
%  sudo service nginx restart
Job for nginx.service failed. See "systemctl status nginx.service" and
"journalctl -xe" for details.
% sudo systemctl status nginx.service
nginx.service - A high performance web server and a reverse proxy
server
   Loaded: loaded (/lib/systemd/system/nginx.service; enabled;
   vendor preset: enabled)
   Active: failed (Result: exit-code)
  Process: 10144 ExecStop=/sbin/start-stop-daemon --quiet --stop -
-retry QUIT/5 --pidfile /run/nginx.pid (code=exited,
status=0/SUCCESS)
  Process: 10112 ExecStart=/usr/sbin/nginx -g daemon on;
master_process on; (code=exited, status=0/SUCCESS)
  Process: 10297 ExecStartPre=/usr/sbin/nginx -t -q -g daemon on;
master_process on; (code=exited, status=1/FAILURE)
 Main PID: 10113 (code=exited, status=0/SUCCESS)
Mar 10 17:59:27 server systemd[1]: Starting A high performance web
server and a reverse proxy server...
Mar 10 17:59:27 server nginx[10297]: nginx: [emerg] "listen"
directive is not allowed here in /etc/nginx/nginx.conf:75
Mar 10 17:59:27 server nginx[10297]: nginx: configuration file
/etc/nginx/nginx.conf test failed
```

I specifically collected the message from a modern systemd-enabled machine to make it a little more confusing. You will deploy on a systemd-based distribution with high probability sooner or later. Please see the highlighted line for the actual reason. Nginx is wonderful in many ways, and reporting its start errors is definitely one of them.

Investigating lower than usual traffic

This case seems to be easier on the business and it might be, but it is actually much worse for you because you don't know what is still working and what is not. Maybe you have an electronic bookstore and all your **Order now** clicks are failing. Everything else works, but you earn only on successful orders. Unfortunately, this is the hardest case of all. On the other side, these are rare.

A common (human) error is letting your HTTPS certificates expire. The parts of your website that are not behind HTTPS will continue to work. Moreover, each browser allows a user to override the expiration warning and go on with the business. Because of this, you will see a number of successful responses in your monitoring and logs, but it will be significantly lower than your usual levels.

Issuing new certificates is easy. You may also try switching HTTPS off for a short while in a desperate attempt to serve some more people while you are waiting for your new certificates. We cannot recommend that.

 Journal: Monitor certificate expiration. This is very easy and will save you from a very unprofessional mishap.

One of the more interesting reasons that you may see lower traffic is performance problems, and we have a whole chapter devoted to performance coming next.

Summary

This chapter outlined a simple process of several steps that allows you to work around many classes of website failures. You might be an experienced system administrator and still benefit from the information because it allows a systematic approach. It may be a seed of your own checklist for example. Anyway, Nginx is a beautiful tightly focused piece of software with an unusually low failure rate. We hope that this chapter and the whole book help you achieve your goals of stability with Nginx. The next chapter focuses on the performance of Nginx.

4

Optimizing Website Performance

One of the most popular reasons to migrate to Nginx is striving for better performance. Over the years, Nginx has acquired a certain reputation of being a silver bullet, a speed beast. Sometimes, this reputation may harm the project, but it is definitely earned. In many situations, that is exactly what happens: you *add* Nginx to a website setup as if it is a concoction ingredient and the website magically becomes faster. We will not explain the basics of how to set up Nginx because you probably know it all pretty well. In this chapter, we are going to delve a little into why this happens and what are the less-known options that will help you squeeze more out of your website.

We will cover these topics in the chapter:

- How Nginx processes the requests
- Nginx caching subsystems
- Optimizing the upstreams
- Some new Nginx features such as thread pools
- Other performance issues

The overwhelming majority of all performance problems people have with Nginx-powered websites are actually on the upstreams. We will try to at least mention some of the methods you may use to tackle the challenge of optimizing your upstream application servers, but we will concentrate on the Nginx itself mostly. You will have to understand the inner workings of Nginx and reverse proxying in general, and we are devoting a good part of the chapter to explain the principles implemented in Nginx that let it run around other older web servers in terms of performance.

The bad news is that you probably won't be able to optimize Nginx very much. If you embarked on a project of making your website sufficiently, significantly faster, and started with inserting Nginx between the application and the users, then you have probably already done the most important steps in moving towards your goal. Nginx is extremely optimal in the sense of avoiding doing extra, unneeded work, and that is the core of any optimization.

Still, some of the configuration defaults may be too conservative for the sake of compatibility, and we will try to talk about this.

Why Nginx is so fast?

The question is intentionally formulated in an oversimplified way. This is what you might hear from your boss or client—let us migrate from old technologies to Nginx because it will make our website faster and users happier. The migration process is described in thousands of online articles and even some books, and we will not write about it here. Many of our readers have probably gone down that path several times and know the facts: first, it is usually true that websites get faster and second, no, it is not usually a full migration. You will rarely dispose of Apache completely and plug Nginx in its place. Although this "total conversion" also happens, most of the time you start with inserting Nginx between Apache and the Internet. To understand why this is okay, why this helps at all, and how to move forward from there, read on.

To describe the main conceptual change that is implemented by using Nginx as a reverse proxy we will use, for simplicity, the processing model of Apache 1.x, that is, a very old piece of software written in premultithreading traditions. The latest Apache version, which is 2.x, may use another, slightly more efficient model, which is based on threads instead of processes. But in comparison to Nginx, those two models look very similar, and the older one is easier to understand.

This is a simple diagram of how one HTTP request-response pair is processed:

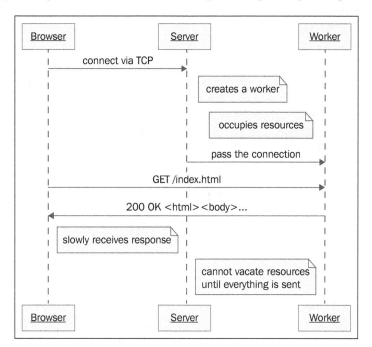

Here is an explanation of the diagram:

1. A user's browser opens a connection to your server using TCP.

2. A web server software that runs on your server and listens to a particular set of TCP ports, accepts the connection, dedicates a part of itself to processing this connection, separates this part, and returns to listening and accepting other incoming connections. In the case of the Apache 1.x model, the separated part is a child process that has been forked beforehand and is waiting in the pool.

3. There are usually some limits in place on how many concurrent connections may be processed and they are enforced on this step. It is very important to understand that this is the part where scaling happens.

4. This dedicated part of the web server software reads the actual request URI, interprets it, and finds the relevant file or any other way to generate the response. Maybe that would even be an error message; it doesn't matter. It starts sending this response into the connection.

5. The user's browser receives the bytes of the response one by one and generates pixels on the user's screen. This is actually a real job and a long one. Data is sent over hundreds of kilometers of wires and optical fiber, emitted into the air as electromagnetic waves and then "condensed" by induction into current again. From the viewpoint of your server, most of your users are on excruciatingly slow networks. The web server is literally feeding those browsers large amounts of data through a straw.

There is nothing that could be done to solve the fifth point. The last mile will always be the slowest link in the chain between your server and the user. Nginx makes a conceptual optimization on step 2 and scales much better this way. Let us explain that at a greater length.

Due to slow client connections, a snapshot of any popular website server software at any particular moment in time looks like this: a couple of requests that are actually processed in the sense that there is some important work being done by the CPU, memory, and disks and then a couple of thousands of requests for which all processing is done, responses are already generated and are very slowly, piece by piece inserted into the narrow connections to the users' browsers. Again, this is a simplified model, but still very adequate to explain what actually happens.

To implement scaling on step 2, the original Apache 1.x uses a mechanism that is very natural for all UNIX-based systems — it forks. There are some optimizations, for example, in the form of having a pool of processes forked beforehand (hence, the "prefork" model), and Apache 2.x may use threads instead of processes (also with pregenerated pools and all), but the idea is the same: scaling is achieved by handling individual requests to a group of some OS-level entities, each of which is able to work on a request and then send the data to the client. The problem is that those entities are rather big; you don't just need a group, but more like a horde of them, and most of the time, they do a very simple thing: they send bytes from a buffer into a TCP connection.

Nginx and other state machine-based servers significantly optimize step 2 by not making big, complex OS-level processes or threads do a simple job while hogging the memory at the same time. This is the essence of why Nginx suddenly makes your website faster — it manages to slowly feed all those thousands of very bandwidth-limited client connections using very little memory, saving on RAM.

An inquisitive reader may ask the question here about why adding Nginx as a reverse proxy without removing Apache still saves memory and speeds up websites. We believe that you already should have all the knowledge to come up with the correct answer for that. We will mention the most important part as a hint: the horde of Apaches is not needed anymore because Apache only does the response generation—the smartest and hardest thing—while offloading the dumb job of pushing bytes to thousands of slow connections. The reverse proxy is acting as a proxy client on behalf of all the users' browsers with the very important distinction: this client is sitting very close to the server and is capable of receiving the bytes of the response lightning fast.

So, the secret sauce to Nginx's performance is not its magical code quality (although it is written very well), but the fact that it saves up on system resources, mostly memory, by not making huge copies of data for each individual request it is processing. Interestingly enough, modern operating systems all have different low-level mechanisms to avoid excessive copying of data. Long gone are times when `fork()` literally created a whole copy of all code and data. As virtual memory and network subsystems get more and more sophisticated, we may end up with a system where the state machine as a model to code tight event-processing loops won't be needed any more. As of now, they still bring noticeable improvements.

Optimizing individual upstreams

You may remember from previous chapters that Nginx has two main methods of generating a response to a request, one being very specific—reading a static file from the filesystem, and the other including a whole family of the so-called upstream modules. An upstream is an external server to which Nginx proxies the request. The most popular upstream is `ngx_proxy`, others are `ngx_fastcgi`, `ngx_memcached`, `ngx_scgi`, and so on. Because serving only static files is not usually enough for a modern website, upstreams are an essential part of any comprehensive setup. As we mentioned in the beginning of this chapter, upstreams themselves are usually the reason why your website has performance troubles. Your developers are responsible for this part because this is where all the web application processing happens. In the following sections, we are going to briefly describe the major stacks or platforms used to implement business logic on the upstream behind Nginx and the directions you should at least look in for clues about what to optimize.

Optimizing static files

Any web application will contain static resources that do not change and do not depend on the user currently using the application. Those are usually known as static files in webmaster parlance and consist of all the static images, CSS, JavaScript, and some other extra data, for example, `cross-domain.xml` files that are used by access control policies of the browsers. Serving the data directly from the application is usually supported to facilitate simple setups without any frontend, intermediate, accelerating server such as Nginx. Nginx's built-in HTTP proxy will happily serve them, and in the case of local caching, may even do that without any noticeable performance loss. However, such a setup is not recommended as a long-term solution if you strive for maximum performance.

One universal step that we feel the need to recommend (or remind of) is moving as much of the static data from the upstream under the control of Nginx. It will make your application more fragmented, but it will also be a very good performance optimization method trumping many of other potential and much harder to implement methods. If your upstreams serve static files, then you need to make them available as files to Nginx and serve them directly. This might be the first thing you do when you receive a new legacy upstream to optimize. It is also a very easy task to accomplish yourself or implement as a part of the whole deployment process.

Optimizing PHP backends

For several years, the modern way to run PHP applications behind Nginx front is the PHP-FPM or FastCGI Process Manager. As you may guess, it uses the FastCGI protocol and will require FastCGI upstream module in Nginx. However, when dealing with inherited legacy PHP websites, you may still meet the older ways of running the code, which will be your first candidates for optimizations.

There is the official Apache way using the `mod_php` Apache module. This module embeds PHP interpreter directly into (each and every!) Apache process. Most of the time, you will inherit Apache websites configured to run in this way. The main good side of embedded interpreters is well known—the code may be saved in some intermediate form between requests and not reinterpreted every time. The `mod_php` Apache module does that wonderfully and some people call it the single reason why PHP gained popularity on the Web in the first place. Well, the way to deal with `mod_php` in 2016 is getting rid of it, together with Apache.

Many PHP codebases can be moved from `mod_php` to PHP-FPM almost effortlessly. After this, you will change your main Nginx upstream from HTTP proxying to directly speaking FastCGI protocol with your PHP scripts that are kept running and ready by the FPM.

Sometimes, your developers will need to invest some resources into mostly restructuring and refactoring code to be runnable in a separate process without any help from Apache. One particularly difficult case is a code that relies heavily on calling into the Apache internals. Fortunately, this is not nearly as common in PHP codebases as it was in the mod_perl codebases. I will mention dealing with Perl-based websites later.

Another really old (and odd) way to run PHP is CGI scripts. Each and every web administrator did or will write a fair amount of temporary CGI scripts. You know, the kind of temporary scripts that live on and on through generations of hardware, managers, and business models. They rarely power parts of production that are user-oriented. Anyway, CGI was not popular with PHP at all because of the ubiquity and rather good quality of mod_php and Apache. Nevertheless, you may have some in your legacy, especially if that code had or has some chances to run on Windows.

CGI scripts are executed as separate processes for each request/response pair and therefore are prohibitively expensive. The only upsides of using CGI are increased compatibility with other Apache modules and another degree of privilege separation. Those are trumped by the performance compromises in all but the most exotic scenarios. By the way, Nginx will make a CGI-powered portion of your website significantly better by buffering the output and releasing the resources on the backend. You still have to plan the rewrite of those parts to be run as FastCGI under FPM as soon as possible.

PHP-FPM uses the same prefork model as does Apache 1.x and that renders some of the familiar knobs under your control. For example, you may configure the number of working processes FPM starts, the upper limit of the requests that may be processed by one child, and also the size of the available child processes pool. All those parameters may be set via the php-fpm.conf file, which is usually installed directly in /etc and following a good convention includes /etc/php-fpm.d/*.conf.

Java backends

The Java ecosystem is so huge that there is a whole bookshelf devoted solely to different Java web servers. We cannot delve deeper into such a topic. If you as an administrator have never had any experience with Java web applications, you will be happy to know that most of the time, those apps run their own web servers that do not depend on Apache. This is a list of popular Java web servers that you may encounter inside your upstreams: Apache Tomcat, Jetty, and Jboss/WildFly. Java applications are usually built on top of huge and comprehensive frameworks that employ a web server as one of the components. Your Nginx web accelerator will talk to the Java upstream via normal HTTP protocol using the ngx_proxy module. All the usual ngx_proxy optimizations apply, therefore. See a note on caching later in this chapter for examples.

There is little you can do to make a Java application perform better without getting your hands dirty deep inside the code. Some of the steps available from the level of system administration are:

1. Choosing the right JVM. Many Java web servers support several different Java Virtual Machine implementations. The HotSpot JVM from Oracle (Sun) is considered one of the best, and you will probably start with that. But there are others; some of them are commercially available, for example, Azul Zing VM. They might provide you with a little performance boost. Unfortunately, changing JVM vendor is a huge step prone to incompatibility errors.

2. Tuning threading parameters. Java code is traditionally written using threads that are a native and natural feature of the language. JVMs are free to implement threads using whatever resources they have. Usually, you will have a choice of using either operating system-level threads or the so-called "green threads," which are implemented in userland. Both approaches have advantages and disadvantages. Threads are usually grouped into pools, which are preforked in a fashion that is very similar to what Apache 1.x does with processes. There are a number of models that thread pools use to optimize both memory and performance, and you, as administrator, will be able to tune them up.

Optimizing Python and Ruby backends

Python and Ruby both built their strength as more open and clear alternatives to Perl and PHP in the age when web applications were already one of the dominant way to deploy business logic. They both started late and with a clear goal of being very web-friendly. There were both the mod_python and mod_ruby Apache modules that embedded interpreters into the Apache web server processes, but they quickly went out of fashion. The Python community developed the **Web Server Gateway Interface (WSGI)** protocol as a generic interface to write web applications regardless of deployment options. This allowed free innovation in the actual web server space that mostly converged on a couple of standalone WSGI servers or containers (such as gunicorn and uWSGI) and mod_wsgi Apache module. They all may be used to run a Python web application without changing any code.

So, it was very natural that Nginx developed its own WSGI upstream module, ngx_wsgi, which you should use to replace any other WSGI implementation. The actual migration path may be a little bit more complex. If the backend application used to run under Apache + mod_wsgi, then, by all means, switch to ngx_wsgi immediately and ditch Apache. Otherwise, for the sake of smoothness and stability, you may start with a simpler ngx_proxy configuration and then move to ngx_wsgi.

You may also encounter an application that uses long-polling (named Comet sometimes) and WebSockets, and runs on a special web server, for example, Tornado (of the FriendFeed fame). These are problems mostly because synchronous communication between the web server and the clients defeats the main advantage of Nginx as an accelerating reverse proxy—the part of the server that processes a request won't be made available quickly for another request by handling the byte pushing to the Nginx frontend. Modern Nginx supports proxying both Comet requests and Web Sockets, of course, but without any acceleration that you may have gotten used to.

The Ruby ecosystem went a slightly different way because there was (and still is) a so-called killer app for Ruby, that is, the Ruby on Rails web application framework. Most of the Ruby web applications are built on Ruby on Rails, and there was even a joke that it is high time to rename the whole language Ruby on Rails because nobody uses Ruby without those Rails. It is a wonderfully designed and executed web framework with many revolutionary ideas that inspired a whole wave of rapid application development techniques throughout the industry. It also decoupled the application developers from the problems of deploying their work by providing the web server that could be shared on the Internet right away.

The current Ruby on Rails preferred deployment options are either using Phusion Passenger or running a cluster of Unicorn web servers. Both options are fine for your task of migrating to Nginx. Phusion Passenger is a mature example of providing its own in-process code as it contains modules for both Apache and Nginx web servers. So, if you are lucky, you will switch from one to the other effortlessly. Passenger will still run worker processes outside of your main Nginx workers, but the module allows Nginx to communicate freely. It is a good example of a custom upstream module. See `https://www.phusionpassenger.com/library/deploy/nginx/deploy/ruby/` Passenger guide for the actual instructions. Passenger may also run in the standalone mode exposing HTTP to the world. That is also the way Unicorn deploys Ruby applications. You know the way to deal with that—the universal helper `ngx_proxy`.

Optimizing Perl backends

Perl was the first widely used server-side programming language for the Web. We may say that it is Perl that brought the notion of dynamically generated web pages to popularity and paved the way for the web applications galore we experience today. There are still plenty of Perl-powered web businesses of various sizes, from the behemoths such as `https://www.booking.com` to smaller, feisty, ambitious startups such as DuckDuckGo. You might also have seen a couple of MovableType-powered blogs. This is a professional blogging platform developed by SixApart and then resold several times.

Perl is also the most popular language to write CGI scripts, and that is also the single reason why it is considered slow. CGI is a simple interface to run external programs from inside a web server. It is rather inefficient because it usually involves forking an operating system-level process and then shutting it down after a single request. This model plus the interpreting nature of Perl means that Perl CGI scripts are so suboptimal that they are used as a model of inefficient web development platforms.

If you have a user-facing, dynamic web page generated by a CGI script run from Apache, you have to get rid of it. See below for details.

There are a number of more advanced ways to run Perl code in production. Partly inspired by the mod_php success, there is a long-running project named mod_perl, which is an Apache module embedding the Perl interpreter into Apache processes. It is also highly successful because it is stable and robust, and powers a lot of heavily loaded websites. Alas, it is also rather complex, both for the developer and the administrator. Another difference from the mod_php Apache module is that mod_perl failed to provide strong separation of environments, which is vital for the virtual hosting businesses.

Anyway, if you have inherited a website based on mod_perl, you have several options. First, there might be a cheap way to move to the PSGI or FastCGI models that will allow you to get rid of Apache. The module Apache::Registry,which emulates a CGI environment inside mod_perl, may be a great sign of such situation. Second, the code may be written in a way that couples it tightly with Apache. The mod_perl module provides an interface to hook deeply into Apache's internals, which while providing several interesting capabilities for the developer, also makes it much harder to migrate. The developers will have to investigate the methods used in the software and make a final decision. They may decide to leave Apache + mod_perl alone and continue to use it as a heavy and over-capable process manager.

Moving CGI to mod_perl nowadays is never a good way forward, we do not recommend it.

There are a number of FastCGI managers for Perl that are similar to PHP-FPM described earlier. They all are very lucky options for you as the Nginx administrator because most of the time the migration will be smooth and easy.

One of the interesting recent modes to run Perl code in web servers is the so-called **Perl Server Gateway Interface (PSGI)**. It is more or less a direct port of Rack architecture from the Ruby stack to Perl. It is interesting that PSGI was invented and implemented in the world where Nginx was already popular. Therefore, if you have a web application that uses PSGI, it was most probably tested and run behind Nginx. No need to port anything. PSGI might be the most important target architecture to upgrade CGI or the mod_perl applications.

Bigger Perl web frameworks usually have a number of ways to run the applications. For example, both Dancer and the older Catalyst provide the glue scripts to run the same application as a separate web server (which you might expose to the world with the help of the Nginx `ngx_proxy` upstream), as a `mod_perl` application or even as a CGI script. Not all of those methods are suitable for production, but they will definitely help in migration. Never accept "we should rewrite everything from scratch" as a recommendation from the developers before weighing other options. If the application was written during the last 3–4 years, it should definitely have PSGI implemented directly or via its framework.

PSGI applications are run with the help of special PSGI servers, such as Starman or Starlet, that speak simple HTTP to the outside world. Nginx will use the `ngx_proxy` upstream for such applications.

Using thread pools in Nginx

Using asynchronous, event-driven architecture serves Nginx well as it allows to save up on the precious RAM and CPU context switches while processing thousands and millions of slow clients in separate connections. Unfortunately, event loops, such as the one that power Nginx, easily fail when facing blocking operations. Nginx was born on FreeBSD, which has several advantages over Linux, and one of the relevant ones is a robust, asynchronous input/output implementation. Basically, the OS kernel is able to not block on traditionally blocking operations like reading data from disks by having its own kernel-level background threads. Linux, on the other hand, requires more work from the application side, and very recently, in version 1.7.11, the Nginx team released its own thread pools feature to work better on Linux. You may find a good introduction into the problem and the solution in this official Nginx blog post at `https://www.nginx.com/blog/thread-pools-boost-performance-9x/`. We will provide an example of the configuration you may use to turn on thread pools on your web server. Remember that you will only need this on Linux.

To turn on background threads that will perform blocking input/output operations without stalling the main loop you use the directive `aio` in this way:

```
server {
    location /file {
        root /mnt/huge-static-storage;
        aio threads;
    }
}
```

You may know the `aio` directive that is used to turn on the Async IO interface, so it is a natural fit for its use to be extended this way.

The implementation is rather simple to explain from a very high level. Transparently to you, Nginx will run a number (pool) of background, userland-level threads that fulfill the input/output tasks. Nginx will continue to run the main event loop in parallel to waiting for the slow disk or the network.

The caching layer of Nginx

If there is one universally known and acclaimed algorithm to speed things up, it is caching. Pragmatically speaking, caching is a process of not doing the same work many times. Ideally, each distinct computational unit should be executed once. This, of course, never happens in the real world. Still, techniques to minimize repetitions by rearranging work or using saved results are very popular. They form a huge discipline named "dynamic programming."

In the context of a web server, caching usually means saving the generated response in a file so that the next time when the same request is received; it could be processed by reading this file and not computing the response again. Now please refer to the steps outlined in the first section of this chapter. For many of the real-world websites, the actual computing of the responses is not the bottleneck; transferring those responses to the slow clients is. That's why the most efficient caching happens right in the browser, or as developers prefer to say, on the client side.

Emitting caching headers

All browsers (and even many non-browser HTTP clients) support client-side caching. It is a part of the HTTP standards, albeit one of the most complex to understand. Web servers do not control client-side caching to full extent, obviously, but they may issue recommendations about what to cache and how, in the form of special HTTP response headers. This is a topic thoroughly discussed in many great articles and guides, so we will mention it shortly, and with a lean towards problems you may face and how to troubleshoot them.

In spite of the fact that browsers have been supporting caching on their side for at least 20 years, configuring cache headers was always a little confusing, mostly due to the fact that there are two sets of headers designed for the same purpose, but having different scopes and totally different formats.

There is the `Expires:` header, which was designed as a quick and dirty solution and also the new (relatively) almost omnipotent `Cache-Control:` header, which tries to support all the different ways an HTTP cache could work.

This is an example of a modern HTTP request-response pair containing the caching headers. These are the request headers sent from the browser (here Firefox 41, but it does not matter):

```
User-Agent:"Mozilla/5.0 (X11; Ubuntu; Linux x86_64; rv:41.0)
Gecko/20100101 Firefox/41.0"
Accept:"text/html,application/xhtml+xml,application/
xml;q=0.9,*/*;q=0.8"
Accept-Encoding:"gzip, deflate"
Connection:"keep-alive"
Cache-Control:"max-age=0"
```

Then, the response headers are:

```
Cache-Control:"max-age=1800"
Content-Encoding:"gzip"
Content-Type:"text/html; charset=UTF-8"
Date:"Sun, 10 Oct 2015 13:42:34 GMT"
Expires:"Sun, 10 Oct 2015 14:12:34 GMT"
Server:"nginx"
X-Cache:"EXPIRED"
```

We highlighted the parts that are relevant. Note that some directives may be sent by both sides of the conversation. The browser sent the `Cache-Control: max-age=0` header because the user pressed the *F5* key. This is an indication that the user wants to receive a response that is fresh. Normally, the request will not contain this header and will allow any intermediate cache to respond with a stale but still nonexpired response.

In this case, the server we talked to responded with a gzipped HTML page encoded in UTF-8 and indicated that the response is okay to use for half an hour. It used both mechanisms available, the modern `Cache-Control:max-age=1800` header and the very old `Expires:Sun, 10 Oct 2015 14:12:34 GMT` header.

The `X-Cache: "EXPIRED"` header is not a standard HTTP header, but was also probably (there is no way to know for sure from the outside) emitted by Nginx. It may be an indication that there are, indeed, intermediate caching proxies between the client and the server, and one of them added this header for debugging purposes. The header may also show that the backend software uses some internal caching.

Another possible source of this header is a debugging technique used to find problems in the Nginx cache configuration. The idea is to use the cache hit or miss status, which is available in one of the handy internal Nginx variables as a value for an extra header, and then you are able to monitor the status from the client side. This is the code that will add such a header:

```
add_header X-Cache $upstream_cache_status;
```

Nginx has a special directive that transparently sets up both standard cache control headers, and it is named `expires`. This is a piece of the `nginx.conf` file using the `expires` directive:

```
location ~* \.(?:css|js)$ {
  expires 1y;
  add_header Cache-Control "public";
}
```

The pattern uses the so-called noncapturing parentheses, which is a feature first appeared in Perl regular expressions. The effect of this regexp is the same as that of a simpler `\.(css|js)$` pattern, but the regular expression engine is specifically instructed not to create a variable containing the actual string from inside the parentheses. This is a simple optimization.

Then, the `expires` directive declares that the content of the `css` and `js` files will expire after a year of storage. The actual headers as received by the client will look like this:

```
Server: nginx/1.9.8 (Ubuntu)
Date: Fri, 11 Mar 2016 22:01:04 GMT
Content-Type: text/css
Last-Modified: Thu, 10 Mar 2016 05:45:39 GMT
Expires: Sat, 11 Mar 2017 22:01:04 GMT
Cache-Control: max-age=31536000
```

The last two lines contain the same information in wildly different forms. The `Expires:` header is exactly one year after the date in the `Date:` header, whereas `Cache-Control:` specifies the age in seconds so that the client can do the date arithmetics itself.

The last directive in the provided configuration extract adds another `Cache-Control:` header with a value of `public`. What this means is that the content of the HTTP resource is not access-controlled and therefore may be cached not only for one particular user but also anywhere else. A simple and effective strategy that was used in offices to minimize consumed bandwidth was to have an office-wide caching proxy server. When one user requested a resource from a website on the Internet and that resource had a `Cache-Control: public` designation, the company cache server would store that to serve to other users on the office network.

This may not be as popular today due to cheap bandwidth, but because history has a tendency to repeat itself, you need to know how and why `Cache-Control: public` works.

The Nginx `expires` directive is surprisingly expressive. It may take a number of different values. See this table:

`off`	This value turns off the Nginx cache headers logic. Nothing will be added, and more importantly, the existing headers received from upstreams will not be modified.
`epoch`	This is an artificial value used to purge a stored resource from all caches by setting the `Expires` header to "**1 January, 1970 00:00:01 GMT**".
`max`	This is the opposite of the "epoch" value. The **Expires** header will be equal to "**31 December 2037 23:59:59 GMT**", and the **Cache-Control max-age** set to 10 years. This basically means that the HTTP responses are guaranteed to never change, so clients are free to never request the same thing twice and may use their own stored values.
Specific duration	An actual specific duration value means an expiry deadline from the time of the respective request. For example, `expires 10w`. A negative value for this directive will emit a special header `Cache-Control: no-cache`.
`"modified" specific time`	If you add the keyword "modified" before the time value, then the expiration moment will be computed relatively to the modification time of the file that is served.
`"@" specific time`	A time with an @ prefix specifies an absolute time-of-day expiry. This should be less than 24 hours. For example, Expires @17h;.

Many web applications choose to emit the caching headers themselves, and this is a good thing. They have more information about which resources change often and which never change. Tampering with the headers that you receive from the upstream may or may not be a thing you want to do. Sometimes, adding headers to a response while proxying it may produce a conflicting set of headers and therefore create unpredictable behavior.

The static files that you serve with Nginx should have the `expires` directive in place. However, the general advice about upstreams is to always examine the caching headers you get and refrain from overoptimizing by setting up a more aggressive caching policy.

The corporate caching proxy configuration that we described earlier in this chapter together with an erroneous `public` caching policy on nonpublic resources may result in a situation where some users will see pages that were generated for other users behind the same caching proxy. The way to make that happen is surprisingly easy. Imagine that your client is a book shop. Their web application serves both public pages with book details, cover images, and so on and private resources with recommendation pages and the shopping cart. Those will probably have the same URL for all users and once, by mistake, declared as `public` with the expiration date in the distant future, they may freely be cached by intermediate proxies. Some more intelligent proxies will automatically notice cookies and either add them to the cache key or refrain from caching. But then again, less sophisticated proxies do exist, and there are a number of reports when they do show pages that belong to other people.

There are even techniques such as adding a random number to all URLs to defeat such caching configurations by making all URLs unique.

We would also like to describe a combination of unique URLs and long expiration dates, which are widely used today. Modern websites are very dynamic, both in the sense of what happens to the document after it is loaded and how often the client-side code changes. It is not unusual to have not only daily but even hourly releases. This is a luxury of the web as an application delivery mechanism, and people seize the opportunity. How to combine rapid releases with caching? The first idea was to code the version into the URLs. It works surprisingly well. After each release, all the URLs change; the old ones start to slowly expire in the cache stores of different levels, whereas the new ones are requested directly from the origin server.

One clever trick was developed upon this scheme, and it uses a hash of the content of the resource instead of the version number as a unique element of the URL. This reduces extra cache misses when a new release does not change all the files.

Implementing this trick is done on the application side. Nginx administrator is only responsible for setting up long expiration date by using, for example, the `expires` `max` directive.

The one obvious thing that limits the effect of the client-side caching is that many different users may issue the same or similar requests, and those will all reach the web server. The next step to never doing the same work many times is caching on the server.

Caching in Nginx upstream modules

Caching infrastructure is implemented as a part of the upstream interface if you excuse us to use object-oriented programming terminology. Each of those upstream modules has a group of very similar directives, which allow you to configure the local caching of responses from that particular upstream.

The basic scheme is very simple—once a request is determined as an upstream material, it is rerouted to the relevant module. If there's caching configured for that upstream, the cache is first searched for an existing response to this request. Only when a cached response is not found, the actual proxying is performed. After this, the newly generated response is saved into the cache while being sent to the client.

It is interesting that while caching on the reverse proxy is known for a while, Nginx gained its fame as a magical accelerator without implementing it. The reason should be evident from the first section—radical changes in RAM consumption alone brought a lot of performance gains. Until the introduction of version 0.7.44, Nginx did not have any caching facilities built in. At that time, web administrators used either the famous squid HTTP proxy for caching or the `mod_accel` module for Apache. By the way, `mod_accel` module was created by Nginx's author Igor Sysoev and turned out to be the testbed for all the ideas about proper reverse proxying that were later implemented in Nginx.

Let us examine the caching directives of the most popular upstream module, `ngx_proxy`. Just to remind, this module hands over the request to another HTTP server. This is exactly how Nginx is run as a reverse proxy in front of Apache, for example. The full description is available in the great Nginx documentation at `http://nginx.org/en/docs/http/ngx_http_proxy_module.html#proxy_cache`. We won't repeat the documentation, but we will provide additional facts and ideas instead.

Directive	Additional information
`proxy_cache_path`	This directive is clearly the main one of the whole caching family. It specifies the storage parameters of the cache store starting with the path on the filesystem. You should definitely familiarize yourself with all the options. The most important are the `inactive` and `max_size` options, which control how the Nginx cache manager removes unused data from the cache store. One required parameter in this directive is the `keys_zone`, which links the cache store to the "zone". See in the later text.

Directive	Additional information
proxy_cache	This is the main switch directive. It is required if you want any caching. It has a single somewhat cryptic parameter named "zone," which will be explained in detail further on. The value "off" will switch the caching off. It may be needed in cases when there is a proxy_cache directive further up the scope stack.
proxy_cache_bypass	This directive allows you to easily specify conditions on which some responses will never be cached.
proxy_cache_key	This directive creates a key that is used to identify objects in the cache. By default, the URL is used, but people add things to it quite commonly. Different responses should never have equal keys. Anything that may change the content of the page should be in the key. Besides obvious cookie values, you may want to add the client IP address if your pages depend on it (for example, use some form of geotargeting via the GeoIP database).
proxy_cache_lock	This is a binary on/off switch defaulting to off. If you turn it on, then simultaneous requests for the same ("same" here means "having the same cache key") resource will not be run in parallel. Only the first request will be executed while the rest are blocked waiting.

The proxy_cache_lock_* family of directives might be interesting when you have some very expensive responses to generate. |
| proxy_cache_lock_age

proxy_cache_lock_timeout | These two specify additional lock parameters. Refer to the documentation for details. |
| proxy_cache_methods | This is a list of HTTP methods that are cacheable. Besides the obvious "GET" and "HEAD" methods, you might want to sometimes cache less popular methods such as "OPTIONS" or "PROPFIND" from WebDAV. There might be cases when you want to cache responses even to "POST", "PUT," and "DELETE" although that would be a very serious bending of the rules and you should really know what you are doing. |
| proxy_cache_min_uses | This numeric parameter with a default value of "1" may be useful to optimize huge cache stores by not caching responses to rare requests. Remember that the effective cache is not the one that stores more but the one that stores useful things that get requested again and again. |

Directive	Additional information
proxy_cache_purge	This directive specifies the additional conditions on which objects are deleted from the cache store before expiration. It may be used as a way to forcefully invalidate a cache entry. A good cache key design should not require invalidation, but we all know how often good designs of anything happen in real life.
proxy_cache_revalidate	This is also a Boolean directive. HTTP conditional requests with headers "If-None-Match" or "If-Modified-Since" may update the validity of objects in the cache even if they do not return any new content to the requesting client. For this, specify "on".
proxy_cache_use_stale	This is an interesting directive that sometimes allows responding with an expired response from the cache. The main case to do this is an upstream failure. Sometimes, responding with a stale content is better than rejecting the request on the basis of the famous "Internal server error". From the user's point of view, this is very often the case.
proxy_cache_valid	This is a very rough cache expiration specification. Usually, you should control the validity of the cached data via response headers. However, if you need something quick or something broad, this directive will help you.

One very important concept that is used in caching subsystems throughout all the upstream modules is that of the cache zone. A zone is a named memory region, which is accessible by its name from all Nginx processes. Readers familiar with the concept of System V-shared memory or IPC via mmap-ed regions will instantly see the similarity. Zones were chosen as an abstraction for the cache state storage, which should be shared between all the worker processes. You may configure many caches inside your Nginx instance, but you will always specify a zone for each cache. You may link different caches to the same zone, and the information about the cached objects will be shared. Zones also act as objects encapsulating the actual cache storage configuration such as where on the filesystem the cached objects will persist, how the storage hierarchy will be organized, when to purge the expired objects, and how to load the objects from disk into memory on restart.

To summarize, an administrator first sets up at least one zone with all the relevant storage parameters with the directive *_cache_path and then plugs subtrees of the whole URL space into those zones with the directive *_cache.

Zones are set up globally, usually in the http scope while individual caches are linked to zones with the simple *_cache directive in the relevant contexts, for example, locations down the path tree or the whole server blocks.

We should remind you that the described caching subsystem directives' family exists for all the upstream modules of Nginx. You will substitute `proxy_` for the other upstream moniker to end up with a whole other family of directives that do exactly the same, maybe with some slight variations for responses generated by upstreams of another type. For example, here for the information on how to cache FastCGI responses at `http://nginx.org/en/docs/http/ngx_http_fastcgi_module.html#fastcgi_cache`.

Let us provide some real-world caching configuration examples that will help you grasp the idea better:

```
http {
    proxy_cache_path /var/db/cache/nginx levels=1:2 keys_
zone=cache1:1m max_size=1000m
inactive=600m;
    proxy_temp_path /var/db/cache/tmp;

    server {
        listen 80;
        server_name example.com;

        location / {
            proxy_pass http://localhost:8080/;
            proxy_cache cache1;
            proxy_cache_valid 200 302 24h;
            proxy_cache_valid 404 5m;
        }
    }
}
```

This is a canonically simple cache configuration with one zone named `cache1` and one cache configured under location / in one server. Several important details are worth mentioning. The temporary files directory configured with the `proxy_temp_path` directive is highly recommended to be on the same filesystem as the main cache storage because otherwise, Nginx will not be able to quickly move files between the temporary and permanent storage and will instead perform an expensive file copy operation.

The `key_zone` size specifies the amount of memory dedicated to the zone. This memory is used to store the keys and metainformation about the objects in the cache and not the actual cached responses (objects). The limit on the object storage is specified in the `max_size` parameter. Nginx spawns a separate process named `cache manager`, which will constantly scan all the cache zones and remove the least used objects when the `max_size` is exceeded.

The `proxy_cache_valid` directive combination specifies a much shorter period of validity for the negative 404 results. The idea behind it is that 404 might actually be fixed, at least some of them may appear due to some misconfiguration. It makes sense to retry such requests more frequently. You should also consider the load on the upstream when making decisions about validity periods. Many computationally heavy search algorithms require much more resources to give a negative answer. It is quite understandable that to make sure that a looked for entity is absent may require checking everywhere instead of stopping after the first found instance. This is a very simplified description of a search algorithm, but it is short enough so that you will remember to always check the request processing time in the logs for negative responses and their relative amount before shortening the cache validity interval.

Two important parameters of the cache are left out in the above configuration, and this means that you will fly with default values. The `proxy_cache_methods` defaults to only caching GET and HEAD requests, which may not be optimal for your web application. And `proxy_cache_key` defaults to `$scheme$proxy_host$request_uri`, which may be dangerous if your web application make similar requests for different users. Read about these directives and either add uniqueness to the key or fall back to uncached behavior via `proxy_cache_bypass`.

Another example that we would like to present is much more complex. Let us devote a separate section to it.

Caching static files

When scaling a website horizontally, you will inevitably find yourself in the situation of having many identical Nginx-powered servers behind a low-level balancer. All of them will proxy the requests to the same upstream server farm, and there will be no problems with synchronizing the active, dynamic content served by your website. But if you follow the advice about having all the static content present locally to allow Nginx to serve it in the most native and efficient way possible, you will end up with a task of having many identical copies of the same files everywhere.

The other way to do the same task is a setup where a farm of Nginx instances is used to serve a huge library of static files, for example, video or music. Having a copy of that library on each Nginx node is out of the question because it is too big.

As usual, there are many possible solutions for these two cases. One choice is having a secondary smaller farm of Nginx servers serving the files to the main farm, which will employ caching inside the `ngx_proxy` upstream.

Another interesting solution uses a network filesystem mounted on the nodes. The traditional Unix NFS has a bad reputation, but in reality, on current Linux kernels, it is stable enough to be used in production. Two of the alternatives are AFS and SMBFS. The files under the mount point will look local to Nginx, but they will still be downloaded over the network, which is much slower than reading a good, local SSD. Luckily, modern Linux kernels have the ability to locally cache files from the NFS and AFS. It is named FS-Cache and uses a separate userland daemon, `cachefilesd`, to store local copies of files from a network filesystem. You may read about FS-Cache at `https://people.redhat.com/dhowells/fscache/FS-Cache.pdf`.

FS-Cache configuration is rather straightforward, and we will not focus on it. There is another way to do it, which follows the philosophy of Nginx much more closely. SlowFS is a third-party, upstream-like module for Nginx, which provides a simple interface to a filesystem subtree. The interface includes caching capabilities, which are standard to all other Nginx upstreams.

SlowFS is open source under a very permissive license and is available either from the author's website or directly from GitHub as a repository. Refer to `http://labs.frickle.com/nginx_ngx_slowfs_cache`.

Here is an example SlowFS configuration:

```
http {
    slowfs_cache_path /var/db/cache/nginx levels=1:2
    keys_zone=cache2:20m;
  slowfs_temp_path /var/db/cache/tmp 1 2;
    location / {
        root /var/www/nfs;
        slowfs_cache cache2;
        slowfs_cache_key $uri;
        slowfs_cache_valid 5d;
    }
}
```

This configuration installs a transparent caching layer over files available locally in `/var/www/nfs`. It does not matter how these files are actually stored, they still will be cached according to the parameters specified with the `slowfs_*` family of directives. But obviously, you will only note any speed-up if `/var/db/cache` is much faster than `/var/www/nfs`.

Replacing external redirects with internal ones

As modern frontend frameworks grow more and more complex, there is an alarming rise in the number of the so-called client-side redirects. Nginx has a great facility that will allow you to save some traffic and precious client waiting time on client redirects. First, let us briefly refresh your knowledge of those redirects.

All the HTTP responses are documents consisting of three principal parts:

*   There's the HTTP code (200: Ok, 404: Not found, and so on)
*   There are a number of loosely structured key-value pairs in the form of headers
*   There is a relatively large, opaque, optional body

There is a lot of good HTTP response codes documentation on the Internet (and also some hilarious pieces given at `http://httpstatusdogs.com/`) — the ones that are relevant to our discussion are in the fourth hundred, that is, between 300 and 399.

Responses with those codes are indications that a browser should immediately make another request instead of the original one. This is why they are called redirects. The semantic differences between various 3xx codes are less important here.

What is important is that many redirects are superfluous. HTTP clients (for example, browsers) spend time on redirects that serve no particular reason besides cleaning up the URL in the address bar. Does Yahoo really need to redirect me from `yahoo.de` to `ru.yahoo.com`, `www.yahoo.com`, and `https://www.yahoo.com` by making my browser issue three additional requests that could easily be avoided? If a website under your control does such things, you may address the question to the respective developers. You may also suggest an easy fix; see later in the text.

There is a cool, little web service that allows you to see the redirects chain as well as some other metainformation that may be useful for debugging. It may be referred to at `https://httpstatus.io/`.

You may go and check whether some of your websites make unneeded redirects, which may cost your slow mobile users' precious seconds before they actually get to the content of your site.

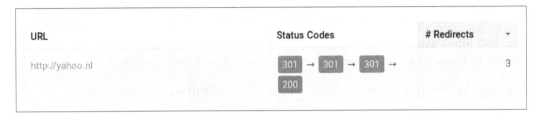

Nginx has a feature named "internal redirects". The idea is that all the intermediate HTTP request-response pairs are processed right inside the server. The client gets the content from the end of the chain in response to the original request. There are a number of methods to enable internal redirects in Nginx, but probably the most flexible is the X-Accel-Redirect response header that an upstream behind Nginx may generate.

For the internal redirects to work with this method, you will have to change the configuration of your upstream software. Instead of generating true redirects via HTTP 3xx response codes coupled with the Location: response header, you will have to generate the earlier-mentioned X-Accel-Redirect: header. This is literally the only change you will have to make. There are a number of places where you need to be careful; all of them concerning the security model of the browsers. The geographic redirects as shown with the Yahoo! example are actually quite rare nowadays, so optimizing them may not be worth the troubles you will get by issuing cookies on the wrong domain. But the example.com to www.example.com redirects are still very popular and look like perfect candidates for internal redirects.

Summary

In this chapter, we discussed several approaches to finding performance problems in your Nginx installation. We mostly focused on working with legacy websites that you might have inherited and are optimizing. The reason for this is that Nginx in itself rarely has any specific problems with being fast enough.

As an operations specialist, you increased your value for the business by gaining knowledge on how to speed up existing working websites having load and customers but based on some pre-Nginx technologies that were a limiting factor.

5
Troubleshooting Rare Specific Problems

The most interesting problems you may encounter with Nginx or any other piece of complex software (or any other human endeavor, for that matter) are usually firmly situated in the category of "Misc". This dreaded class of troubles contains everything that does not fall into other convenient classes that you as a reader and a professional spent time and efforts in previous chapters. Nginx is known for its stability and robustness, so you might never get a chance to encounter anything we describe here in your professional career. Still, in the spirit of "better safe than sorry", we would highly recommend reading the chapter just in case.

In this chapter, you will learn about the following topics:

- Different security warnings that users may encounter on your websites and how to fix them

- A couple of reasons why users may see very obsolete versions of web pages that were updated and how to fix such cases

- Several curious configuration problems that will help you better understand the inner workings of Nginx and how to solve them

Anyway, let us start from what we consider more frequent and easier to fix and then move to less obvious and much more obscure issues.

Security warnings

It is a fact that the web is moving to HTTPS. Even 3 – 4 years ago, plain text HTTP was a perfectly normal choice unless you build a bank interface. Today, in the age of global personalization and sophisticated attackers, websites are slowly embracing total encryption. There are a number of reasons for that, and deep discussion is out of the scope of this book. Instead, you are kindly referred to this document `https://www.eff.org/encrypt-the-web-report`. Basically, in the next 2-3 years, HTTP will become de facto deprecated as an end user protocol and that brings us to a world of problems dealing with the public key infrastructure of HTTPS. HTTPS relies on TLS, which uses X.509 PKI with CAs, CRLs, OSCP, and so on. The abundance of abbreviations in the previous sentence is deliberate; this is a complex topic in itself, which regularly confuses the most experienced specialists. The design of the X.509 key and certificate infrastructure is known to be very complex, but the task it solves is not a simple one either. One of the most interesting recent initiatives to simplify the solution is the project **Let's Encrypt**, which is available at `https://letsencrypt.org`. They advertise as the free certificate vendor (certification authority, or CA in X.509 lingo), but they also provide a set of protocols, services, and tools which allow painless and transparent certificate management. They are not yet fully operational as of March 2016, so watch that space.

Setting up HTTPS on Nginx is a topic thoroughly described in many articles and books around the web, so we won't spend much time on it. You have probably done it several times.

There are some cases in which your visitors may encounter HTTPS-related security warnings when requesting pages from your website.

Let's say that you have something like this in your website configuration:

```
listen 443 ssl;
ssl_certificate
"/site/example.com/conf/https_public_cert.pem";
ssl_certificate_key
"/site/example.com/conf/https_priv.key";
```

When the X.509 infrastructure was invented in the end of 1980s, one of the tasks it tried to solve was the issue of mutual authentication and trust between parties in a secure communication channel. While encryption does not strictly require this kind of authentication, it is still considered important that your browser trusts the server on the other side of an encrypted HTTPS connection at least in the sense of that server presenting some undeniable proof that it is what it claims to be. The implementation of that proof are the digital certificates that servers present while negotiating the connection, and a number of policies on a client. Amusingly, if you are familiar with other PKI schemes, for example, PGP/GPG, then you probably asked yourself why X.509 requires a separate entity in addition to the obvious key pair (public and private), which is actually required to implement asymmetrical cryptography. Well, the idea is that the certificate is a document from a third party about the server, whereas the keys are technical data used during encryption. The loose PGP analog of the certificate are the signatures from other people your keys may or may not have.

Domain name mismatch

The most common certificates HTTPS server use are of **Domain Validation** (DV) type, and the most important policy that a client will enforce against a connection to a server with a DV certificate is that the domain name mentioned inside the certificate matches the domain name of the actual TCP connection endpoint.

A problem with this policy manifests itself with these nasty scary full-screen errors:

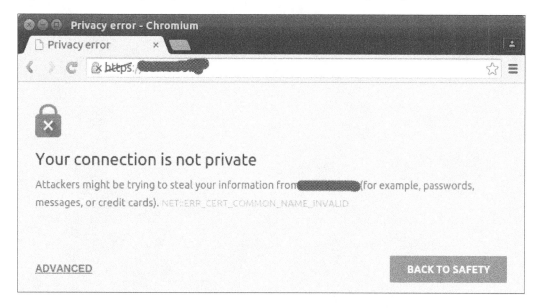

The earlier-mentioned image is from Chromium, the open browser that is the base for Google Chrome. The next example is from Firefox:

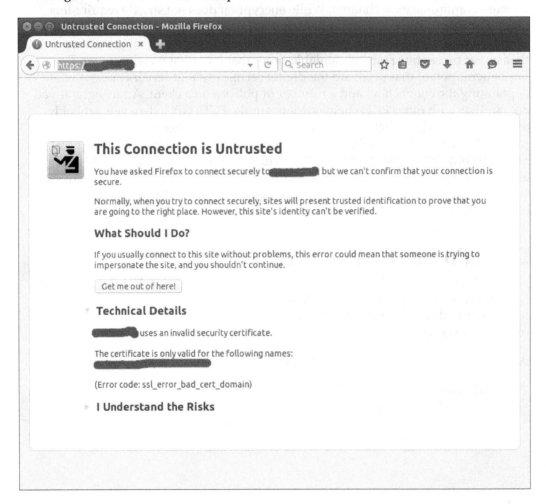

The next example is from mobile Safari on iOS:

The root of this problem lies in the historic convention of having one and only one fully qualified domain name per certificate. If you have aliases (and most websites usually do have at least the common pair — one with "www." and one without "www."), you either have to purchase separate certificates or use extensions to the original X.509. Fortunately, those extensions are pretty widely supported; the last problems we remember were with default Windows Phone 7 browsers, and if you have significant number of such clients, you probably know what to do and have resources to solve that problem with a dedicated project.

The extensions you need are: wildcard certificates and multidomain certificates or SAN certificates. Your HTTPS certificates vendor will have those in store. They are usually a bit more expensive but too useful to ignore. Wildcard certificates allow you to request certificates for domain patterns that look like `*.example.com`, whereas **Subject Alternative Names (SANs)** are a way to enumerate the list of domains that this certificate is valid for.

Expired certificates

The next most common error message that you may encounter is as follows:

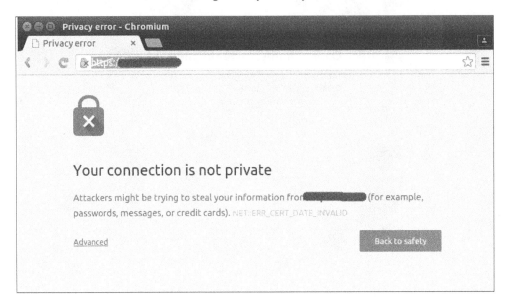

Now we will show Chromium and Microsoft Internet Explorer errors as examples:

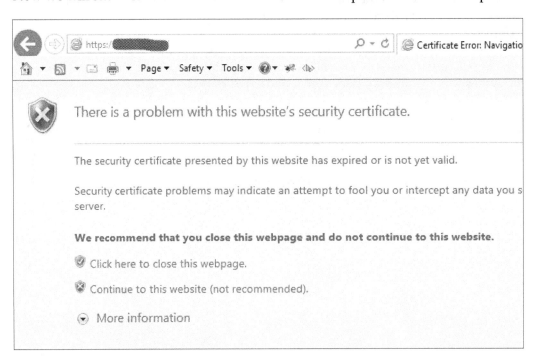

iOS and Mobile Safari chose the strategy to show one type of HTTPS error message for both of the most common errors.

The philosophy behind digital certificate expiration is rather simple. Because a certificate is an electronic document asserting someone's identity as verified by a third party (that is your certificates vendor or **Certificate Authority (CA)** in X.509 speak) in the absence of said third party, it should have expiration date to ensure regular re-evaluations of that identity. Vendors will go out of their way to remind you about your certificates, but in spite of this, expirations happen a little too often in the wild.

This is a very embarrassing moment for any system administrator responsible for a web server. Almost as embarrassing as forgetting to renew the domain delegation (this also happens a lot). Most of the monitoring solutions, both standalone and hosted, will have a sensor for that. We even found a specific monitoring tool just for certificate expiration at `https://snitch.io/` although we have not had the chance to use it. One of the most robust tools to ensure that your TLS certificates are renewed on time is, surprisingly, Google Calendar. Acquire the habit of always creating an event with a reminder 4 weeks before the expiration date right after you receive each new certificate file. This will save you, we promise.

You may ask how a problematic certificate could end up in production. Well, most of the time, production certificates are not used on development and test deployments because of the old convention mentioned earlier — having one domain name per certificate. Because this limit is long obsolete, you may include your test hostnames inside certificates and that will remove one additional difference between your production and test (or stage, depending on your release life cycle) environments.

Insecure warnings for valid certificates

There are hundreds of different Certificate Authorities (CAs) now; some of them worked for many years and some are just starting. If you had time to get familiar with X.509 PKI, you will know that clients should have the root certificate for each and every issuer (that is, CA) in their trusted storage. Otherwise, all the server certificates issued by that particular CA will be invalid. In an ideal world, all user computers and mobile devices have a very up-to-date list of trusted root certificates. Unfortunately, an ideal world does not exist, and you may face a real problem when some of the more conservative clients' browsers consider your web servers insecure because they do not yet have the relevant CA root certificate in their trusted storage.

To work around such problems, your CA may provide you with their own certificate that you should concatenate with your own and present to the clients as a certificate set (or chain). This will work because X.509 supports a certificate chain to verify the endpoint certificate. Your certificate will refer to the CA certificate, which if provided will refer the client further down the chain until one of the referred intermediate CA certificates is found in the trusted root certificate storage of the client.

The easiest way to do this is with a simple `cat` command:

```
$ cat your_example_domain.pem CA.pem > certs.pem
```

Then, specify the path to this compound file in your `ssl_certificate` directive.

The mixed – content warning

Although the two types of HTTPS problems we demonstrated earlier are true errors and web browsers will actively prevent users from working around them, there are some less critical problems that still may compromise the trust of your clients.

One of the most massive and, at the same time, elusive warnings is the so-called "Mixed content" warning. The idea is that any HTTPS page should never embed HTTP objects because the overall security level of the page is the level of its least secure component. If you have even one image object that was fetched via plaintext HTTP, then it may compromise the whole page and even the whole application at times. All modern browsers give warnings about this situation although the actual interface implementation may vary.

These are some examples. The first one is from a desktop version of Firefox:

The second example is from a desktop version of Chromium:

Also, modern browsers make a distinction between active and passive content, the former including scripts, active objects, such as Flash, style sheets, and whole external documents as IFrames. Active mixed content is usually blocked outright, whereas passive mixed content only issues warnings. There is a recommendation from W3C about "Mixed content" that contains all the best practices and recommendations about handling the issue. You may well use it as a guide about what to expect. Refer to `http://www.w3.org/TR/mixed-content/`.

Linking insecurely to your own content is an obvious error on the side of the developers. They should never ever use direct absolute links with the `http:` scheme anymore. Fixing this may be quite easy using a couple of global full-text searches through all the documents and templates. Just ensure that all your secondary hosts are reachable via HTTPS and change `http://` in links to either `https://` or just `//` if you feel like saving a few bytes per link by using a clever trick of schemeless (or schemaless) URLs. A URL without a scheme looks like the following:

```
<img src="//img.example.com/images/face.png">
```

The idea exploits a rarely used but required by all standards feature of relative URL resolution. This is also the reason for the second name: protocol-relative. URLs with two slashes will inherit the scheme from the base document. Refer to RFC3986 `http://tools.ietf.org/html/rfc3986#section-4.2` for more information.

 It will be more secure and practical in the long run to just ensure HTTPS availability and always use `https://` instead of `//`. It is completely safe and does not decrease (already absent) security of your documents retrieved via insecure HTTP.

As a workaround solution (that may become semi-permanent), you may use the power of Nginx to help your developers change all links to internal resources using on-the-fly substitution. Nginx source contains a special module named `ngx_http_sub_module`, which is not usually built by default although it depends on the author of the Nginx package in your distribution. To check whether it is available, run this command:

```
$ nginx -V 2>&1 | fgrep -c http_sub_module
1
$
```

If you see `1`, then your Nginx is linked with `sub_module`. Otherwise, you need to compile it using `--with-http_sub_module` parameter to `configure`.

This is the example that you will need to modify for your own situation:

```
location /path {
    sub_filter_last_modified on;
    subs_filter_types text/css;
    sub_filter ' src="http://img.example.com'  '
src="https://img.example.com';
    sub_filter ' href="http://img.example.com'  '
href="https://img.example.com';
}
```

The second line with `sub_filter_types` directive is only needed if your CSS files contain absolute URLs of images. It is as dirty a hack as many `sub_module` applications are, but it may solve at least some of the immediate problems you have. Remember to include all your assets hosts.

There are two main sources of insecure external content your website may contain. The first includes external trackers, advertisement networks, commenting systems, and the like. In 2016, all of these have the support for HTTPS websites. The only reason they may the mixed content warnings is incorrect embedding code (for example, very old).

The other source of insecure objects is **User-generated Content (UGC)**. If your website has a way for users to post some data that may be displayed in the context of your pages afterwards, then you might have this problem. Examples include commenting systems, blogs, forums, messaging, and so on. This is not as rare as it might seem at first thought.

One way to find the culprits of the mixed content violation is using the browser console. Recent browsers display warnings about which objects are insecure. There are also tools for crawling websites and identifying insecure embeds, but these may not be relied upon, especially if you have a complex website that may not be easily crawled. Refer to, for example, `https://www.whynopadlock.com/` or `https://www.jitbit.com/sslcheck/`.

Mozilla provides a good page on Mixed Content too. You are very welcome to consult it at `https://developer.mozilla.org/en-US/docs/Security/MixedContent`.

While fixing the embedding code of external components is rather straightforward, dealing with UGC content is much harder. Suppose that you have a way for your users to specify their image avatars by entering URLs pointing to those images. You cannot just change the URL from `http:` to `https:` because this may just break the link. You cannot be sure that all those far-away hosts support and will always support HTTPS. The only way to provide such a service for your own users is to serve all that remote content yourself by proxying it.

This is an important hack that involves some of the less popular Nginx magic and requires collaboration with your developer team, but in the end, you will have a very efficient proxy for the external content. Brace yourself.

Building a secure proxy for the external content

Here is an example of a simple but relatively secure proxy for external images. It may be extended to other types of content with ease.

The relevant part of Nginx configuration looks like this:

```
server_name proxy.example.com;
location @1.gif {
  empty_gif;
}

location / {
  proxy_cache ext_images_cache;
  proxy_cache_valid 200 48h;
  proxy_cache_valid 301 302 304 404 1h;
  secure_link_secret "some-secret";
  if ($secure_link = "") {
    return 403;
  }
  set $proto "http";
  if ($uri ~ "/secure/")
  {
    set $proto "https";
  }
  image_filter_buffer 10M;
  image_filter test;
  proxy_connect_timeout 5;
  proxy_read_timeout 5;
  proxy_send_timeout 5;
  proxy_ignore_headers Expires Cache-Control X-Accel-Redirect X-Accel-Expires;
  proxy_intercept_errors on;
  proxy_pass $proto://$secure_link;
  error_page 301 302 401 403 404 415 500 501 502 503 504 505 =200 @1.gif;
  access_log /var/log/nginx/cache/access-secure.log proxy;
}
```

It uses several Nginx modules to implement resources that look like:

```
https://proxy.example.com/insecure/5f814704a38d9bc1915fd19fa0c7a00a/
images.external.com/image.gif
```

The prefix "insecure" may also look like "secure" and encodes the protocol part of the original URL. When requested, this URL will either generate the response from a local cache or request an external image via HTTP, cache it locally, and send to the client.

The first named location block provides a fallback, that is, an empty 1 x 1 image that we will serve on all invalid requests.

The second big location block anchored at / is the main configuration. Since we have a dedicated hostname for the proxy, we work right from the root. First, there are declarations of caching and secure link parameters. After checking the validity of the request by using a condition on $secure_link variable, we compute the original, source URL schema or protocol. We use /secure/ as the prefix for HTTPS, and any other prefix will mean simple insecure HTTP.

A couple of image_filter_* directives configure the image filter to only ever check the first 10 megabytes. Proxy timeouts provide us with reasonably robust HTTP client. We do not want to hang endlessly on very slow (or maliciously slow) servers while also processing those servers that are not as fast as everyone hopes.

The interesting parts of the configuration are the secure link and image filter functionality that employ ngx_http_secure_link and ngx_http_image_filter modules, respectively.

The image filter module is the simpler of the two. It runs several heuristic checks against the contents of an image file to ensure that it is indeed a GIF, PNG, or JPEG image. This protects from several of the older browser security bugs that could be exploited with specially crafted responses masquerading as images. See http://nginx.org/en/docs/http/ngx_http_image_filter_module.html for more information.

The secure link module checks the cryptographic signature in the URL. The idea is that without the signature, you will create an HTTP proxy open to the whole world, which is a helpful resource for malicious actors of all kinds. The signature should be generated on the application side by your development team. The algorithm is described in the module documentation at http://nginx.org/en/docs/http/ngx_http_secure_link_module.html.

This module has a second, even more secure mode of operation that will also check the signature for expiration. We recommend that you implement that one too, see the documentation for details. The example mentioned earlier uses the easiest possible mode for the sake of brevity.

This proxy is not a final solution that we usually install in production but a simple version. For example, it does not properly process redirected images. As you may see from the last lines, many HTTP response codes including those 3xx that are responsible for redirects are considered errors and get redirected to an empty GIF. A solution for that is a good exercise in the Nginx configuration.

Solving problems with cache

We spent a lot of time on providing good caching, that is, saving intermediate results and serving saved copies instead of recalculating from scratch for the same requests. This works perfectly only in a perfect world (for example, a pure functional world where functions and, by extension, GET/HEAD HTTP requests do not have side effects). In the real world, two equal requests may sometimes lead to different responses. There are two basic reasons for it: the earlier-mentioned side effects, which change the state despite the perceived idempotence of GET/HEAD, or flawed equality relationship between requests. A good example of this is ignoring wall time when the response depends on it.

Such problems usually manifest themselves as complaints about seeing stale versions of some pages on your website or seeing pages that belong to other users. Although you can tolerate the first type to some extent (for example, as a compromise for performance), the second type is a major offense and a blocker for the operation of your business.

The hunt for the misbehaving caches is a process that involves the same two sides that we discussed in the previous chapter. The caching may happen both inside Nginx as the effect of the caching upstream directives and on the side that is closer to the client—either the very browser that initiated the request or one of the intermediate caching proxies. The effect of the client-side caches is usually smaller these days, so it is safer to start switching it off first. You need to have this directive in all scopes:

```
expires -1;
```

Any negative value will work. This instructs Nginx to emit `Cache-Control: no-cache` HTTP response header alongside the content. It will effectively break client-side caching with a couple of caveats. First, we do not have direct control of those caches, of course, and they are free to comply with the standards of the modern web at will. For example, they may be configured to ignore `no-cache` in an ill-advised attempt to save on traffic. The authors personally debugged a couple of cases of such overzealous frugality, and it was a nightmare. And, second, even fully compliant caches may lag because to receive the `no-cache` instruction they need to reach the origin server while actively trying to avoid that, which is the whole point of caching.

The second step in this troubleshooting process is switching off the caching inside Nginx upstream caches. As was explained in the previous chapter, each Nginx upstream has a family of directives that configure caching for this particular upstream connection. The main switch for the whole mechanism is the `*_cache` directive. In the case of `ngx_fastcgi` upstream, the directive looks like this:

```
fastcgi_cache zone;
```

Here, the `zone` is an identifier of the so-called cache zone, which is basically a collection of caching configuration or caching profile. To switch caching off, you will use the fixed zone name `off`.

It will take immediate effect (the common cycle of `nginx -t` and then `sudo service nginx reload`, or analog for your distribution should be second nature by this time), but it may also devastate your actual application upstream by significantly increasing the incoming request rate. Be aware of that. You may take smaller steps in troubleshooting the cache by using the `*_cache_bypass` or `*_cache_valid` directives in a smart way. The first one provides a way to skip caching some of the responses altogether, and the second is a quick-and-dirty way to limit the age of the entries in the cache.

The `*_cache_valid` directive does not override the expiration parameters set via HTTP response headers from the upstream application. So for it to be effective, you will also need to remove those headers with a `*_ignore_headers` directive first.

Again, the asterisk here means the actual upstream type; in the case of FastCGI upstream you will use `fastcgi_cache_valid` and `fastcgi_ignore_headers` directives. The simple example will look like this:

```
fastcgi_ignore_headers "X-Accel-Expires" "Expires" "Cache-
Control";
fastcgi_cache_valid 1m;
```

It will force caching all the responses for 1 minute. Unfortunately, it will also cache the responses that the upstream does not intend to be cached because Nginx will also ignore `Cache-Control: no-cache` in this configuration. Be careful not to leave your troubleshooting session in production.

Obsolete pages and VirtualBox

There is one other possible problem that manifests itself as users (or, more frequently, developers) seeing old versions of web pages in HTTP responses. There is a bug in VirtualBox virtualization software, which is very popular as a development virtualization solution (for example, with Vagrant or, more lately, Otto). VirtualBox is also sometimes used as a production virtualization technology. It has a feature named "shared folders", which allows it to have a copy of the host machine folder inside one of the guest machines.

The bug is in the handling of the `sendfile()` Linux kernel syscall inside VirtualBox. This syscall directly copies a file to a TCP socket, avoiding extra unneeded memory copies and providing all possible optimizations for this rather specific but very popular special case. You can imagine how well this case suits many Nginx workloads. Even if it is not just serving local static files, Nginx cache may use `sendfile()` very efficiently.

The support for `sendfile()` is conditional and may be switched off using this directive:

```
sendfile off;
```

It is highly recommended if you run Nginx inside VirtualBox and serve files from a shared folder.

Apache migration problems

One of the Apache features that Nginx chose not to replicate is the support for the so-called `.htaccess` files. Those files were invented as a way to easily configure access control for individual virtual hosts in a virtual hosting environment where clients are only able to see their own subfolders via the magic of `chroot` (often called from ftpd). The implementation is rather simple; this is an autoincluded piece of configuration that Apache constantly monitors for changes. Not every possible Apache configuration directive is allowed in `.htaccess` (but many of them are, essentially, all that do not require a restart).

This feature was (ab)used as a convenient way to distribute the relevant web server configuration inside the source code for a website or a web application. Although the idea is still relevant, the Apache implementation with a silent change monitoring and transparent reconfiguration is not considered well designed. So, instead of the proper .htaccess support, Nginx suggests to explicitly include site-specific configuration files and then reload the configuration.

If your website source directory contains some .htaccess files, chances are that you will need to manually convert the directives into either a section inside the main nginx.conf or a separate file, which is to be included from nginx.conf.

One particular case is the proliferation of Apache mod_rewrite directives inside the .htaccess files. This will give you a hard time in the general case because Nginx uses a very different language for the URL rewriting functionality. One especially difficult case is the web apps that modify their own rewrite rules in .htaccess as part of their normal workload. Unfortunately, you have to either run an instance of Apache for them or order the rewrite of the relevant parts of their code altogether.

Here is an example of some old Apache rewrite rules:

```
RewriteEngine on
RewriteCond %{HTTP_REFERER} !^$
RewriteCond %{HTTP_REFERER} !^http://(www\.)?example.com/.*$ [NC]
RewriteRule \.(gif|jpg|png)$ http://www.example.com/dummy.gif [R,L]
```

The idea here was to break the so-called hotlinking – a practice when images were directly embedded in external documents, and this web host sent the bytes without getting any real users.

The same logic could be implemented for Nginx using these directives:

```
location ~ \.(jpe?g|png|gif)$ {
    if ($http_referer ~ "^$") {
        return 301 http://www.example.com/dummy.gif;
    }
    if ($http_referer !~ "^http://(www\.)?example\.com") {
        return 301 http://www.example.com/dummy.gif;
    }
}
```

Although Nginx actually contains a special module for referrer checking, it will do the same job in a much more elegant way. Refer to the following:

```
valid_referers none blocked example.com *.example.com;
if ($invalid_referer) {
    return 301 http://www.example.com/dummy.gif;
}
```

The logic of long chains of the Apache `mod_rewrite` rules poorly translates into Nginx. You should rethink the tasks and try to implement the solutions using more elegant ways that Nginx provides, such as `try_files` or special modules. See also `http://nginx.org/en/docs/http/converting_rewrite_rules.html`.

There are several tools to help convert static sets of the Apache `mod_rewrite` directives into the Nginx syntax. In our practice, they are all only partially useful and always require human fixes in the end. You may look at `http://winginx.com/en/htaccess`.

By the way, this tool does not handle the earlier-mentioned example with the HTTP Referrer properly.

Solving problems with WebSockets

WebSockets are a modern protocol that allows a web application to have persistent, duplex, long-living connections to servers, similar to real TCP connections (and they are, under the hood, pretty normal TCP connections).

WebSockets use the special URL scheme `ws://` (or `wss://` for secure), and you will see that in your browser error console if you try to run a WebSocket-opening web application from an Nginx-powered server.

The philosophy behind WebSockets directly conflicts with the buffered-reverse proxy idea that is the foundation of Nginx as a web accelerator. See the previous chapter for the comprehensive introduction into what makes Nginx fast. Fortunately, modern Nginx is so much more than just a simple reverse proxy. It has so much to offer that even without the buffering and cheap connection pools, it is too valuable to ditch because of WebSockets. And since version 1.3.13, which was released almost 3 years ago, in early 2013, Nginx has had special support to create long-living tunnels between the client and the server, which was specifically introduced to support WebSockets.

To enable upgrading a normal HTTP connection to a WebSocket, you have to do this:

```
proxy_pass http://localhost:8080;
proxy_http_version 1.1;
proxy_set_header Upgrade $http_upgrade;
proxy_set_header Connection "upgrade";
proxy_read_timeout 1000s;
```

You should appreciate how the support was introduced without a single new directive. The configuration language is already rich enough for this. The magic happens due to the `Upgrade:` header sent by the client and the `101 Switching Protocols` HTTP response code from the server.

One very important parameter is the timeout specified with the `proxy_read_ timeout method`. The default value of 1 minute might not be sufficient for your (and most other) WebSocket use cases. The whole idea of direct long-living connections between the app in the browser and the server may be defeated by a short proxy timeout. It is perfectly normal for a WebSocket connection to be idle for long periods of time, and this is the reason for the increased timeout value. The other solution is implementing some sort of heartbeats or pings between the sides of the connection.

Showing a file upload progress bar

Uploading files from the web browser to the server is a rather common feature of modern web applications. Any number of CMS or publishing systems allows users to upload images to include these with their textual content, as shown in the following image:

Here is an example of a web upload in progress. The basic idea behind one of the algorithms to implement the progress bar is to initiate a POST request in an IFrame and then poll some well-known URL for the progress counter. Modern browsers allow us to get the progress information right on the client's side; this is a part of XMLHttpRequest Level 2 and was standardized about 3 years ago. There are a lot of older web applications that still rely on the older methods.

The described method only works if your client-side posts to your server-side with the same speed that the user actually sees in their interface. The problem is Nginx that buffers the long POST and then quickly and efficiently pushes it to the server-side code. The progress-poller process will not be able to get any progress until the very last moment when suddenly the entirety of the upload process happens in an instant.

There are several solutions to it. A dirty workaround is to process the uploads that you want to show progress for outside of Nginx. That is, have a backend server that is directly connected to the Internet, POST all your files to it, and get your progress from it.

A much better solution is to spend some resources and reimplement the progress bar part of the interface to use progress events available in modern browsers. The JavaScript (with jQuery + jQuery Form plugin) code will look as simple as this:

```javascript
$(function() {
    var bar = $('.progress_bar');
    var percent = $('.percentage');
    var status = $('#status');

    $('form').ajaxForm({
        beforeSend: function() {
            status.empty();
            var percentVal = '0%';
            percent.html(percentVal);
            bar.width(percentVal);
        },
        uploadProgress: function(event, position, total,
        percentComplete) {
            var percentVal = percentComplete + '%';
            percent.html(percentVal);
            bar.width(percentVal);
        },
        complete: function(xhr) {
            status.html(xhr.responseText);
        }
    });
});
```

A somewhat strange, middle-ground solution would be to use the `nginx_uploadprogress` module, which provides its own progress reporting endpoint. The example configuration will look like this:

```nginx
location / {
    proxy_pass http://backend;
    track_uploads proxied 30s;
}

location ^~ /progress {
    report_uploads proxied;
}
```

The client side will have to mark all the POSTs to the / location with a special header or GET parameter X-Progress-ID, which may also be used to get the progress of that particular upload via the /progress resource.

Solving the problem of an idle upstream

We devoted a great deal of content to the concept of upstreams. Just to remind you, upstreams are entities that generate HTTP responses that Nginx sends to the clients. Usually, an upstream contains several (or at least one) servers speaking one of the supported protocols, such as FastCGI or plain HTTP. Nginx uses sophisticated client code to very efficiently proxy the communication between the clients and the upstream in a transparent way by also optimizing the number of idle connections and wasted memory. There are a number of algorithms that Nginx uses to balance the client load on all the members of an upstream block, and one of those algorithms is known to bite the unsuspecting web administrators.

The configuration under discussion looks like this:

```
proxy_pass http://backend;

upstream backend {
    server server1.example.com;
    server server2.example.com;
    server server3.example.com;
    ip_hash;
}
```

The first line sets up the handling of some location or the whole server by proxying everything to a named upstream. The mentioned upstream is configured in the block later. It consists of three servers and a special directive ip_hash, which turns on an algorithm to use when choosing one of the three servers that will actually process each incoming request.

The default algorithm is the so-called weighted round-robin. In our simple configuration without any weights, the round-robin would choose the servers one after the other in that order and rewind back to the first after the last. It is an efficient and simple algorithm that will surely balance the load in a good fashion. One significant disadvantage of it is that the requests from the same client may end up being processed on different upstream servers, which sometimes is not good, for example, because of the caching in RAM on the individual upstream servers. The directive ip_hash will turn the round-robin off, and instead, servers will be chosen based on a hash value computed from the IP address of the client.

One of the consequences is that the same client will always talk to the same server (unless that server is down, in which case the hash value will point to another server trying to minimize the effect on the rest of the servers in the upstream). The other consequence is that your client load will be distributed between servers only as evenly as your client IP addresses. Usually, when you have enough load to justify proper upstream blocks with many servers, your client IP pool will already be big and diverse enough. Sometimes there is another proxy in front of Nginx, and all your incoming requests look like they come from a very limited set of addresses. In this case, you have a subtle and hard-to-debug problem, which may or may not lead to a disaster.

If you are lucky, you will note that the load on your upstream servers is very uneven. For example, if one of those three servers is completely idle although there are no problems with it, and it happily responds to direct requests.

The quick and dirty workaround here is to remove the `ip_hash` directive. The proper solution will require you to employ the `ngx_http_realip` module and provide better data for the IP-hashing algorithm. The idea is to save the real client IP address to a special HTTP request header on the proxy that is located in front of the Nginx and then take it from there instead of the real endpoint address of incoming TCP connections. This module may not be compiled in your version of Nginx.

There are also other consistent hashing strategies that you might consider. Refer to the full documentation for hashing at `http://nginx.org/en/docs/http/ngx_http_upstream_module.html#hash`.

Summary

In this chapter, we have provided you with a number of seemingly unconnected cases that you may or may not have the luck to face for real. We have quickly recapped on the most popular troubles with SSL/TLS certificates that webmasters encounter starting from the most embarrassing expiration to building a whole caching proxy for external insecure content. We have also described a number of cases with caching, URL rewriting rules migration, file-upload progress interfaces, and concluded with the mystery of an idle upstream. The next chapter is devoted to building a proper monitoring system for your Nginx-powered servers. We will move from solving problems to actively preventing them.

6
Monitoring Nginx

After reading this chapter you will be able to set up proper monitoring for your Nginx installation using the features freely available as part of base Nginx distribution and several of the more popular monitoring and alerting systems available on the market.

You will also get acquainted with an advanced monitoring solution that is included in the Nginx Plus subscription package, which the makers of Nginx sell as a commercial service.

Knowing what is happening to your web server is the first step towards fixing and preventing any problems. Setting up monitoring and alerting is one of the essential steps in any production deployment, and Nginx web servers are not the exception here. Experienced web administrators will never feel calm enough until they have real-time insight into the performance and load indicators.

There are several sources of data for your monitoring system provided by Nginx. First, there are logs, which you may configure up to your preferences. There is also a number of statistics interfaces available for Nginx that you may enable and connect to various industrial monitoring systems, both free and commercial. The logging subsystem was described in the *Chapter 2, Searching for Problems in Log Files*, which can be referred to for additional information. One particular tool that uses logs to enable online monitoring and debugging should be mentioned.

Using ngxtop

When the first version of the famous Unix utility top(1) was conceived in 1984, imitating an old VMS command that did a similar thing, the author was unlikely to imagine that he actually created a whole class of online system administration tools suited for both routine and emergency situations. Since then, top has become an essential program, and many other utilities have been born with the same principle in mind — produce a dynamic interactive *top N* list of items sorted by a particular criteria. There are `htop`, `iotop`, `mytop`, `pg_top`, `ntop`, `iftop`, and many others. The Nginx ecosystem has its own top, which is named `ngxtop` and is hosted on `https://github.com/lebinh/ngxtop`.

The recommended way to install ngxtop is using the `pip` package manager for Python packages. Your distribution may or may not have `pip` installed by default, so you might also need to install `pip` first. On Debian-based Linux distributions, you will usually be all set up with:

```
$ sudo apt-get install python-pip
```

On a FreeBSD box, you need to install the port `devel/py-pip` with these:

```
$ cd /usr/ports/devel/py-pip
$ sudo make install
```

When `pip` is available, you can install the actual `ngxtop` with it:

```
$ sudo pip install ngxtop
```

You can run `ngxtop` right away, and due to some heuristics, it will correctly locate your main Nginx log all by itself.

This is how the `ngxtop` default output looks like on a simple and rather idle website access log:

```
●●●  root@nymph: /var/log/nginx
root@nymph:/var/log/nginx# ngxtop -l access.log

running for 655 seconds, 1852 records processed: 2.83 req/sec

Summary:
|  count |   avg_bytes_sent |  2xx |  3xx | 4xx |  5xx |
|--------+------------------+------+------+-----+------|
|   1852 |        48249.299 | 1647 |   75 | 130 |    0 |

Detailed:
| request_path                          | count |  avg_bytes_sent |  2xx | 3xx |  4xx | 5xx |
|---------------------------------------+-------+-----------------+------+-----+------+-----|
| /                                     |  1183 |       67672.964 | 1179 |   3 |    1 |   0 |
| /atom.xml                             |   473 |       18929.962 |  401 |  72 |    0 |   0 |
| /favicon.ico                          |    56 |         894.000 |   56 |   0 |    0 |   0 |
| /robots.txt                           |    45 |         153.933 |    0 |   0 |   45 |   0 |
| /trackback/                           |    15 |         134.000 |    0 |   0 |   15 |   0 |
| /index.opml                           |     9 |       30249.000 |    9 |   0 |    0 |   0 |
| /apple-touch-icon-precomposed.png     |     6 |          89.333 |    0 |   0 |    6 |   0 |
| /apple-touch-icon.png                 |     6 |          89.333 |    0 |   0 |    6 |   0 |
| /wp-content/uploads/samplc.php        |     4 |         162.000 |    0 |   0 |    4 |   0 |
| /blog/wp-admin/                       |     2 |         162.000 |    0 |   0 |    2 |   0 |
root@nymph:/var/log/nginx# █
```

There are two tables in the output. The first one shows the summary line. The
columns are pretty obvious. The ones that must catch your attention immediately
are the rightmost two (titled 4xx and 5xx), which contain the counters for the HTTP
requests that led to errors.

The second table is more interesting because it has all the incoming requests
classified by the request path. You may immediately see which paths generate errors,
for example. In the earlier example, you will note that the website lacks the robots.
txt file and also the special high resolution icons, which were first used by the iOS.
The counts in the lower table do not add up exactly to the respective counts in the
top table because the least happening request paths are not included here.

ngxtop has several powerful command-line options, which make it one of the
best tools to analyze a log from a misbehaving website. For example, in *Chapter 2,
Searching for Problems in Log Files*, we described how to create custom log formats
extending the information beyond what a common access logs offer. ngxtop is able to
accept a log format definition and even parse it from the nginx.conf file itself.

The command-line switch for the custom log format is -f. The whole command will
look just like this:

```
$ ngxtop -f  '$remote_addr - $remote_user [$time_local] "$request" '
```

Getting statistics from http_stub_status

Nginx base distribution contains a simple module that provides access to several rather basic but useful counters inside Nginx that are very important to monitor on a regular basis. The module is named `ngx_http_stub_status`, and we will describe how to use it in monitoring.

This module is not compiled by default. To check if your Nginx distribution is compiled with the `stub_status` module, you can use this command:

```
$ nginx -V 2>&1 | fgrep -c http_stub_status_module
1
$
```

If you see `1`, then this module is compiled and linked to your Nginx binary. Otherwise, you need to compile it using `--with-http_stub_status_module` parameter to `configure` script that is invoked during Nginx compilation.

Once you have this module available, you can use its directives (actually, there is only one) in `nginx.conf`. This is an example of `stub-status` sharing:

```
location /stub-status {
    stub_status;
}
```

This module belongs to the family of the so-called content-generating modules, which are able to directly process incoming HTTP requests and generate responses. The other main family of modules that can provide HTTP responses to clients are the upstream modules, which are more complex content generators consulting external resources for the actual data. While we spent a significant amount of time explaining upstreams in previous chapters, content generators were not given so much attention due to their relative simplicity. Some other interesting content-generating modules that are included in Nginx distribution are `ngx_http_empty_gif` and `ngx_http_autoindex`.

The earlier configuration will create a primitive web page as a response to the GET request with the URI of `/stub-status`. You can use any other URI as well. The page will contain several counters. Let's see an example and learn what those numbers mean. A fresh web server after a restart will generate this page:

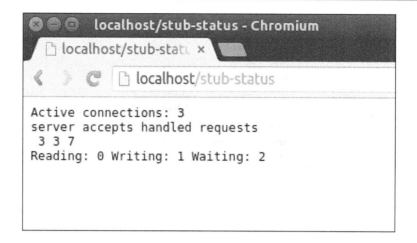

This is not even a web page per se, but just a plain text HTTP response clearly intended to be processed by scripts and not by people:

```
$ curl -si http://localhost/stub-status | fgrep Content-Type
Content-Type: text/plain
$
```

Let's dive deeper into the values that you see in this output:

Parameter name	Description
Active connections	This is the number of all client connections that are being processed right now. This counter is bumped on each successful `accept()` and decreased after each `close()`. The number will also be a sum of reading + writing + waiting.
Server accepts	The global ever-increasing counter of all connections that were `accept()-ed`.
Handled	The counter of all handled connections. Most of the time, this number is the same as the previous one, but some of the connections are closed right after being accepted and they are not counted as handled.
Requests	This is the global counter of all HTTP requests received by this Nginx instance. It may be smaller than the handled counter due to "keep-alive" connections that may receive many requests before closing.
Reading:	This is a snapshot number of all connections that are currently in the process of reading HTTP request headers.

Parameter name	Description
Writing:	This is the number of connections that are in one of the states after the reading of the headers of the request. It may be a little confusing, but connections that are reading the body of the request or communicating with one of the upstreams are counted against this number.
Waiting:	This is the counter of all "keep-alive" connections that are waiting for the next request from the same connected client.

Most of these counters are also available as Nginx variables and can be used in the `log_format` configuration. The module exports these variables:

- `$connections_active`
- `$connections_reading`
- `$connections_writing`
- `$connections_waiting`

The global counts of connections and requests can be restored from the logs without any additional variables.

The only directive from this module is `stub_status`, and its usage pattern is obvious from the earlier example. You can specify it in one of the scopes; most probably, you will choose a location. Older versions of Nginx may require you to specify a parameter like `ok` or `1` for this directive.

While the simplest status content generator may only contain one line with this directive, it is highly recommended to make some additions.

This is the working practical example of `stub_status` configuration:

```
location /stub-status {
stub_status;
    access_log    off;
    allow    $monitoring_ip;
    deny     all;
}
```

The `access_log off` directive will switch off logging for this location. You may want to comment out it while you debug but in the end only your monitoring system will make requests to this path from predefined IP addresses and at predefined intervals. The logging of this regular GET request-response pair will not be very useful while littering the logs with very redundant information.

The third and the fourth lines are about access control. While `stub_status` does not share any particularly confidential information, it may still be valuable to either competitors or malicious actors who plan to attack your infrastructure. A golden rule of not sharing anything by default works here.

To fully understand how we could use the data, let's write a simple manual alerting script using cron. As an example, we will specify the task as follows: once a minute check the requests rate and alert the administrator if the rate per minute exceeds a certain predefined threshold.

The code for the check is given later. It is a simple Perl script that should be called from a crontab with a time specification of */1 * * * *, which means running once every minute. It uses the `PushBullet` service to send alerts. `PushBullet` allows mobile apps and browser extensions to receive those notifications and has a simple HTTP API:

```perl
#! /usr/bin/perl
use strict;
use warnings;

use autodie;
use LWP::Simple;
use WWW::PushBullet;

my $stub_status_url = 'http://localhost/stub-status';
my $threshold = 2000; # requests per minute

my $data_file = '/var/run/req-rate';
my $pb = WWW::PushBullet->new( {
    apikey => '...PushBullet API key...',
});

BEGIN {
    # For LWP inside PushBullet
    $ENV{PERL_NET_HTTPS_SSL_SOCKET_CLASS} = 'Net::SSL';
}

open my $fh, '+<', $data_file;
my ($prev, $prev_ts) = split ' ', scalar <$fh>;

my $reqs;
if (get($stub_status_url) =~ /(\d+)\s+Reading: /s) {
    $reqs = $1;
}
```

```
my $now = time();

if ($prev && $reqs) {
    my $rate = ($reqs - $prev) / ($now - $prev_ts) * 60;
    if ($rate > $threshold) {
        $pb->push_note({ title => 'req rate alert', body => "Requests
per minute: $rate" });
    }
}

seek $fh, 0, 0;
truncate $fh, 0;

say $fh "$reqs $now";
```

The script parses the output of the `ngx_http_stub_status` module with a simple regular expression and compares the global requests counter with the previous value, which it saves in a file. If the increase in the counter divided by the time passed exceeds a constant, it sends an alert. This is the model employed by all monitoring and alerting systems out there.

The next step for us is using the data from this module as a sensor in several monitoring systems that are available on the market. Most of the systems allow comprehensive graphs of all available counters and also custom alerts on events like a value exceeding a threshold of some kind.

Monitoring system	Nginx support plugin
Nagios	`https://exchange.nagios.org/directory/Plugins/Web-Servers/nginx`
Zabbix	`https://github.com/zbal/zabbix/blob/master/scripts/zabbix_nginx_check.sh`
ZTC	`https://bitbucket.org/rvs/ztc/wiki/Home`
Munin	`https://github.com/munin-monitoring/contrib/tree/master/plugins/nginx`
Cacti	`http://forums.cacti.net/download/file.php?id=12676`
Collectd	`https://collectd.org/wiki/index.php/Plugin:nginx`
OpenNMS	`http://www.opennms.org/wiki/Monitoring_Nginx_with_the_HTTP_collector`

Many hosted monitoring solutions, such as DataDog, Scout, New Relic or ServerDensity, support collecting data from the Nginx `http_stub_status` module as well.

Here is how ServerDensity displays data received from Nginx:

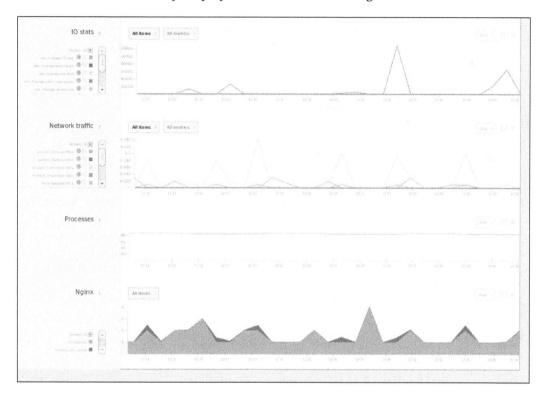

The earlier-mentioned graph will only contain two entities: current client connections and requests per second. You notice that those two come very close to each other, which means that there were no or little keep-alive connections that managed to pass over more than one request.

Monitoring Nginx with Munin

Munin is a free software networking and infrastructure monitoring system. We chose it because the configuration is simple and allows us to demonstrate the principles. You will certainly prefer to use the same monitoring solution that you use for your other needs. If you do not currently use anything that is not very probable, Munin is as good an option as any other to start with.

Munin was developed with easy extensibility via plugins in mind. It uses the famous RRDTool time series database that was first developed as part of MRTG but then found its way to many other free and open source software as the time series database and time-based graphs engine.

Installing Munin is not as easy as we wish it were but the process is thoroughly described in the online Munin guide `http://guide.munin-monitoring.org/en/latest/installation/index.html`. There is also a book about Munin published by *Packt Publishing, Instant Munin Plugin Starter*. It may be a little old but still contains enough relevant information.

Munin is also one of the monitoring systems that has plugins to parse the output from the Nginx `http_stub_status` module in its distribution. The plugins are available right after Munin installation and are supported as part of the release cycle of Munin.

The architecture of many network monitoring systems is very similar to a classic star topology system with a master that is responsible for drawing graphs, watching for events, and issuing alerts based on data provided by agents, each of which represent a host or a service. Munin agents are named nodes and installing Munin usually installs an instance of the Munin node on the same host as well. That sounds absolutely okay as the master host of a monitoring system should definitely be monitored itself. It is the node component that has integration with different software to get metrics that should be monitored. Munin plugins for Nginx are executable scripts that are run as part of the Munin node operation. The node process reports the data from those (and all the other) plugins to the Munin master, which has the interface for the administrators.

After successful installation of Munin, you will find all standard plugins in `/usr/share/munin/plugins` or some other directory depending on your distribution. There are two standard Nginx plugins in Munin 2.0.25 – `nginx_requests` and `nginx_status`. Both of those plugins parse the output of the `http_stub_status` Nginx module and thus require the `url` environment variable to point to the `stub_status` output URL with a sane default of `http://localhost/nginx_status`. To switch the plugins on, you need to link them into `/etc/munin` with a command such as:

```
$ sudo ln -s /usr/share/munin/plugins/nginx_* /etc/munin/plugins/
```

You may also examine the `contrib` Nginx plugins available at `https://github.com/munin-monitoring/contrib/tree/master/plugins/nginx`. These are not installed by default, but are still part of the Munin source tree.

After restarting the Munin node running on the host, the metrics reported by Nginx are immediately available for this particular host. To check whether the plugins can successfully access Nginx and parse its `stub_status`, you can use these convenient commands:

```
$ sudo munin-run nginx_request
request.value 15
$ sudo munin-run nginx_status
total.value 2
reading.value 0
writing.value 1
waiting.value 1
$
```

Given that your Munin master and nodes are running, you will start to get updated graphs for Nginx metrics at once. A clean Munin without any past data will show something like this:

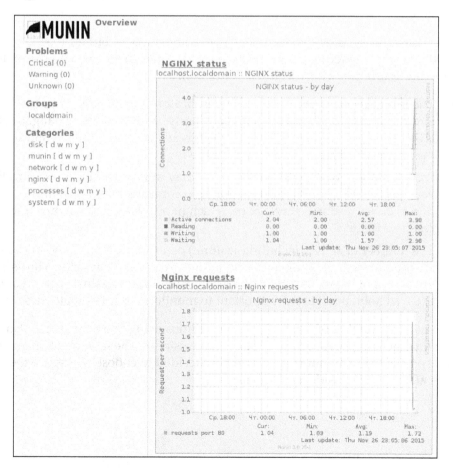

Adding more hosts to the Munin master is completely transparent, provided that those hosts run the node with Nginx plugins. All of the reported metrics will show up instantly and will get drawn and checked against limits, which also brings us to the next topic.

Configuring alerts

Although monitoring itself is a very broad term and as a job may include a lot of activities, there are basically two sides to what a web service monitoring constitutes. Graphing values from sensors is important as a tool to make strategic decisions based on visually apparent trends and also a post factum investigation and sometimes even as a forensics tool. The other side is alerting, which allows administrators to react to incidents as quickly as possible, preventing business consequences. All major monitoring solutions include alerting subsystems and even the toy monitoring script that we built earlier in this chapter is basically a simple alerter.

The `http_stub_status` module provides scarce information, but it can still be used to quickly react to incidents. These are some good values that can be used to detect unusual conditions requiring immediate attention:

- The incoming request rate is a global indicator of the load to your website. Sudden spikes indicate a surge in popularity, which might be dangerous or a **Denial of Service (DoS)** attack, which is always dangerous. A sudden dip may mean a failure, even a total meltdown.

- A high number of dropped connections may indicate that the configuration is not up to the load. Nginx does not drop connections unless it has to due to either resource shortage or, which happens more often, meeting resource limits.

- The number of active (including waiting) connections may sometimes mean an attempt to drain your connection limits by a malicious actor. This is exactly what Nginx usually manages to defend itself against without any external help, but it is still important to monitor and investigate these events.

You can use any number of complex alert conditions using these three and also invent more metrics relevant to your particular business. The method to create such alerts is specific to the monitoring system you decided to choose. These are the example alerts we use inside ServerDensity:

- Munin uses a simple system of two-level thresholds attached to plugins as a way to generate alerts. There are "warning" and "critical" thresholds, and once the actual value reaches one of the thresholds, Munin will generate an alert and send a notification. The system allows default thresholds for all hosts, which may be practical.

- The more popular way is to set up thresholds for all hosts individually. It is done right in the Munin master configuration file, which is called `munin.conf`. This file contains a list of all hosts that are under monitoring by this very master. Adding a threshold for a metric available on a host is as simple as this:

```
[www1.example.com]
    nginx_status.total.warning 0:10
    nginx_status.total.critical 0:20
```

The values are specified as ranges; that is, in the earlier case, the warning would be generated only when the `nginx.status.total` metrics (which is the total number of current connections) will leave the range from 0 to 10.

Munin is able to send notifications about the alerts via e-mail, via syslog, via piping to external programs, or via Nagios, which is another popular monitoring system with a more sophisticated alerting subsystem. Configuration of the notification settings is easy enough. See the online Munin guide at `http://guide.munin-monitoring.org/en/latest/tutorial/alert.html`.

- All of the interesting metrics may be measured right on the front between Nginx and its clients and also on each external link that Nginx has due to upstream configuration. Unfortunately, the open source Nginx does not contain any means to expose those metrics from the upstream links to monitor and set up alerts on.

Getting more status data from Nginx

In this section, we will explore the ways to get more information about an Nginx instance so that the monitoring can be more extensive and cover more details.

In 2014, Nginx creators launched a commercial umbrella company for the open source Nginx software, which started to explore the business models around the server. One of the most anticipated features was comprehensive monitoring and the developers delivered on that front.

The commercial product of Nginx company is named Nginx Plus. It is a subscription service marketed to medium and large businesses already dependent on Nginx for their infrastructure. Nginx Plus pricing is based on yearly licenses per single instance and is rather aggressive, which also means that once you need these features, you already have several instances and need several licenses. For complete and up-to-date information, refer to the Nginx Plus web page at `https://www.nginx.com/products/`.

One of the most important part of the subscription is the availability of the new status module, which is named `ngx_http_status`, and is a kind of elder brother for the open source `ngx_http_stub_status` that most of the monitoring solutions we described depend on.

Along with programmatic access to the status data in machine-readable form, Nginx Plus provides a beautiful and expressive dashboard that you can use without any integration into your enterprise monitoring. The `https://www.nginx.com` team kindly provides a demonstration of what the dashboard can do at `http://demo.nginx.com/status.html`.

The configuration for the `ngx_http_status` module looks like this:

```
location /status {
    status;
}
```

As you can see, it is an almost exact copy of what we did earlier for `stub_status`, but the main directive is now more aptly named `status`. This location will accept a number of different requests. It provides a hierarchy of information about different objects, such as upstreams and cache zones.

The built-in dashboard is actually a one-page HTML application that retrieves all the information it needs from `/status`. The static HTML will be installed with the Nginx Plus distribution. On Debian-based systems, you can find it at `/usr/share/nginx/html/status.html`. To add the dashboard to your Nginx Plus instance, see this configuration example:

```
location = /status.html {
    root /usr/share/nginx/html;
}
```

Having your own Nginx dashboard is never enough because if you invested into Nginx Plus subscription you probably have some business-critical operations and you need automatic monitoring. At the same time, the dashboard is the perfect way to explore the information that is exported by Nginx Plus. The `ngx_http_status` module provides wealth of information in machine-readable format (JSON or JSONP) to integrate with all the systems we mentioned earlier. And using the new metrics available, you will be able to monitor more. Let's dig deeper into what `ngx_http_status` returns by default:

```
$ curl http://localhost/status
{"version":6,"nginx_version":"1.9.4","address":"127.0.0.1","generation":4
,"load_timestamp":1448573854895,"timestamp":1448573864361,"pid":3691,"pro
cesses":{"respawned":0},"connections":{"accepted":208,"dropped":0,"active
":1,"idle":1},"ssl":{"handshakes":0,"handshakes_failed":0,"session_reuse
s":0},"requests":{"total":8309,"current":1},"server_zones":{"localhost_ht
tp":{"processing":1,"requests":12,"responses":{"1xx":0,"2xx":11,"3xx":0,
"4xx":0,"5xx":0,"total":11},"discarded":0,"received":3305,"sent":7756}}-
,"upstreams":{},"caches":{}}
$
```

As you can see, the default output format for this module is JSON, which allows much more complex data structures. The same data re-indented for readability looks like this:

```json
{
    "version":6,
    "nginx_version":"1.9.4",
    "address":"127.0.0.1",
    "generation":4,
    "load_timestamp":1448573854895,
    "timestamp":1448573864361,
    "pid":3691,
    "processes":{
        "respawned":0
    },
    "connections":{
        "accepted":208,
        "dropped":0,
        "active":1,
        "idle":1
    },
    "ssl":{
        "handshakes":0,
        "handshakes_failed":0,
        "session_reuses":0
    },
    "requests":{
        "total":8309,
        "current":1
    },
    "server_zones":{
        "localhost_http":{
            "processing":1,
            "requests":12,
            "responses":{
                "1xx":0,
                "2xx":11,
                "3xx":0,
                "4xx":0,
                "5xx":0,
                "total":11
            },
            "discarded":0,
            "received":3305,
```

```
        "sent":7756
      }
    },
    "upstreams":{ },
    "caches":{ }
  }
```

On the upper level of the return JSON object, we see these items:

version	This is the version of the format of these data. It is important for parsers because some of the items only appeared starting from a specific version, and you may require Nginx upgrade to get enough information for your parser. As of December 2015, the last version of this is 6.
nginx_version	This is the version of Nginx software.
address	This is the IP address of the server generating the status report.
generation	This gets incremented by one each time you reload Nginx configuration. So in a sense, this is the number of the current configuration generation. One may wonder why the generation number is important. One of the reasons is that it may not be practical to compare some indicators, for example, performance if the generation and therefore the configuration has changed.
load_timestamp	The Unix epoch timestamp of the last configuration reload.
timestamp	Current UNIX timestamp.
pid	The process identifier of the worker that processed this specific status request.
processes	This is an object with a single field (it may be extended in future versions of the response structure), which is named respawned, and contains the number of all child processes that we restarted after a failure.
connections	This is an important object containing the information that we otherwise can obtain via the open source ngx_http_stub_status module.
connections.accepted	This value inside the connections object is the total number of all accepted client connections.

`connections.dropped`	This is the total number of dropped connections. Note that with `http_stub_status` module, we have to calculate this value ourselves.
`connections.active`	The number of currently active connections.
`connections.idle`	The number of connections that are idling.
`ssl`	This is also an object with several values inside. Those are SSL (actually, TLS) counters. SSL is an older version of the protocol for encrypted connections. The proper name for the current protocol is TLS, but the old name is still used by some conservative specialists.
`ssl.handshakes`	The total number of TLS handshakes.
`ssl.handshakes_failed`	The total number of unsuccessful TLS handshakes. This is a very interesting and important value that is not available via `http_stub_status` while being rather critical to monitor.
`ssl.session_reuses`	Each TLS handshake is an expensive operation, and there is an optimization that reuses one of the previously established TLS sessions to avoid the handshake altogether. A low number here means an opportunity to increase performance with little investment.
`requests`	An object with two values.
`requests.total`	This is the same number that is printed last on the third line of the `http_stub_status` output. The global counter for all client requests received via all connections.
`requests.current`	The number of currently processed requests.
`upstreams`	If there is one important feature of Nginx Plus that you want to name to justify the purchase, it should probably be the upstreams object in the `http_status` output. It allows the metrics of the individual upstreams and hosts inside upstreams to be monitored. The example host mentioned earlier does not have any upstreams configured, and this is why the object is empty.
`caches`	This object contains the status of all configured caches. Most of the cache configuration is done with the upstream directives.

server_zones	This object is a custom storage that you can fill with data using the status_zone directive inside one of your server blocks. Status zones are a new concept in Nginx Plus. They provide an additional level of flexibility in collecting status data. You can find comprehensive documentation on this directive at http://nginx.org/en/docs/http/ngx_http_status_module.html#status_zone.

Each of the server zones contains a separate multilevel object with the status information collected from all servers connected to the same status zone. That object looks like this:

processing	The snapshot number of currently processed requests.
requests	The total counter of all requests.
responses.total	The number of responses sent to clients. Should be close to the number of requests.
1xx	The number of responses with HTTP 1xx status codes.
2xx	The number of responses with HTTP 2xx status codes.
3xx	The number of responses with HTTP 3xx (usually redirects) status codes.
4xx	The number of responses with HTTP 4xx (usually indicating bad requests that should be fixed on the client side) status codes.
5xx	The number of responses with HTTP 5xx (meaning internal server errors) status codes.
discarded	The number of requests that did not generate responses.
received	Total bytes received from clients.
sent	Total bytes sent to clients.

Using Nginx Plus alternatives

The Nginx Plus commercial subscription gives you more than just the ngx_http_status module. If you do not need the other perks of the Plus version but crave more metrics, you could explore some of the freely available alternatives.

nginx-module-vts

One way to get more information from inside Nginx is this open source module published on GitHub at `https://github.com/vozlt/nginx-module-vts`.

The author was clearly inspired by the official `ngx_http_status` features and even used the same structures and dashboard client-side code (although the older version). This may be actually a good thing because you can start integrating `nginx-module-vts` and then transfer all the scripts with minimal modifications to Nginx Plus once you are ready for the subscription. The documentation is wonderful, and there are many examples. Some of the keys in the JSON objects that are returned by this module differ from the official `ngx_http_status` keys, and because of this, we would recommend abstracting the actual key names in your monitoring configuration files.

Luameter

Another alternative to the great official `ngx_http_status` is the Luameter package, which is a collection of scripts in the Lua programming language that integrates with Nginx using the `ngx_http_lua` module. The format of the data collected and exported by Lua is also clearly inspired by the official and pricey alternative, so you will be able to switch with little effort.

The idea of the very useful `ngx_http_lua` module is to let Nginx administrators hook snippets of custom Lua code into different phases of request processing.

Luameter is distributed on a pay-as-you-go model, so it is not free. The lowest price is just 10 US dollars, so it is very cheap in comparison with what the commercial arm of Nginx sells. Refer to `https://luameter.com/` for all the information about Luameter.

nginx-lua-stats

This is another collection of scripts in Lua. It may be used by itself to collect and export online statistics about the number of generated HTTP responses with various HTTP status codes, but it is even more valuable as an example of using Lua hooks to collect additional data and report it.

The code is published on GitHub at `https://github.com/yandex-sysmon/nginx-lua-stats`.

`nginx-lua-stats` works its magic by setting up a hook on the logging phase, which collects the data, and then setting up another hook on the content generation phase for a particular location which is able to actually generate a full HTTP response with the collected statistics.

Here is the relevant part of the `nginx.conf` file:

```
location /stat {
    content_by_lua_file 'show_stat.lua';
}

location /html {
  log_by_lua_file 'collect_stats.lua';
}
```

The requests to the /stat location will return the collected data. The second location block installs an additional log handler which is actually a counting hook. The effect is that all requests for the documents under /html hierarchy will invoke the collect_stats.lua script as part of the logging phase.

The upsteam_check module in tengine

One of the many advantages of open source development models is the possibility of forks, which are separate versions of the main software with changes that are not accepted by the original author. Sometimes, forks become very successful in their own right and even supersede the original versions. One of the biggest Chinese websites Taobao has its own Nginx fork, which is named tengine. There are a number of big websites beside Taobao that prefer tengine to the original Nginx. Tengine has some rather advanced features for upstream management and monitoring.

The `upstream_check` module allows us to specify some custom health checks for all the hosts in an upstream group. That is an interesting functionality by itself, but it is the secondary feature that got the module in this chapter. The directive `check_status` inside a location is a content generator such as the `status` and `stub_status` of the official modules that we discussed at length in this chapter.

This directive provides a report on the health of different hosts in an upstream group in either human-readable HTML or machine-readable JSON or even CSV format.

See the examples of configuration and output at `http://tengine.taobao.org/document_cn/http_upstream_check_cn.html`.

The requests/sec patch by Catap

There is a patch for a very old Nginx version that adds one very interesting metric to the `ngx_http_stub_status` output. The metric is the requests rate that otherwise may be only approximately calculated using saved past state from the main total requests counter.

The patch is available at `http://catap.ru/patches/nginx/request_per_seconds.dpatch`.

Unfortunately, it does not apply cleanly to modern Nginx source, so you will have to do some manual conflict resolution.

The Ustats module

There is also another piece of rather old code that may or may not be brought up to date with modern Nginx. It is called Ustats, and it is officially put into the "abandonware" category. Such projects may provide a starting point for some in-house development efforts. See `https://github.com/0xc0dec/ustats` for the code and `https://code.google.com/p/ustats/` for some documentation.

Summary

In this chapter, we delved deep into the details of different ways to monitor a working Nginx instance. There is a very useful command-line log parsing utility ngxtop as well as two real-time statistics interfaces, which are available in open source and commercial versions of Nginx, respectively. We went over all the data items that these interfaces expose and discussed the integration options with many monitoring systems available on the market.

The next chapter will conclude the whole book by giving future directions for the reader. It may even seem to contain some career advice. There is also an appendix providing a reference into all the different errors and warnings that you may encounter in your work with Nginx.

7
Going Forward with Nginx

In the modern, interconnected constantly changing world, nothing ends with the last pages of a book, including this one. By the time you read this, some of the new features mentioned will have become wildly popular, and some may start their way to being obsolete. Nginx as open source software with a highly devoted team of developers, vibrant community, and a huge growing install base will have hundreds of changes committed and tested. You may wonder whether there is a sure way to keep up with it. Is it needed at all? While the current fashion moves in the direction of mobile-first, cloud-connected, intelligent Internet of things, the underlying protocols and principles remain. HTTP has long moved beyond anything imagined by its inventors, and it is living through a new circle of evolution with the rapid adoption of HTTP/2 after a long and somewhat controversial period of testing in the form of SPDY. Nginx was, and is, there on the frontlines. There is little doubt that HTTP in one form or another is here to stay for a long time, and it is a safe bet to build a good chunk of your professional career around it, especially when such a wonderful tool is readily available in your kit.

Although the industry of providing Internet services is still young, the main career models are already established. If you love Nginx and have successfully read this book, you basically have two main options for moving forward.

System administration

System administration is the art of combining hardware and software together so that the sum is much more valuable than all of the parts. If you prefer more down-to-earth definitions, system administration is the operations specialist responsible for the technical components of business processes or even more to the point, web servers hosting websites, web applications, and, increasingly, the backend API endpoints. As the industry grew, the difference between software engineering and system administration became more important, and most modern businesses have separate roles for these jobs. There is a reverse trend of the so-called DevOps movement, by the way. DevOps engineers combine the administration (or -ops) skills with software development.

This book is mainly for Nginx administrators who work alongside separate development teams, and it is very natural to want to become better and more valuable at this job. There are several vast fields of knowledge that will make you better at administering web servers.

Linux/Unix operating system as a whole

Linux has long become the de facto standard run web servers, but just being familiar with it is not enough. A deep understanding of all the inner workings may become a great goal in your career. Starting from the file systems, going down to the actual bytes on the disk level, moving to the virtual memory subsystem, to processes, signals, and all the ways interprocess communication works is a long road to perfection that will pay off tremendously when you face a really tricky bug or a vicious attack. We would also recommend looking at other Unix-type free operating systems, mostly FreeBSD and OpenBSD, which are certainly worthy competitors and have a different set of basic principles at their core. They might become your personal favorites and secret weapons. You should intimately know all the processes that Nginx consists of, the way they may be controlled, and the way they communicate between themselves.

Modern Internet protocols

Included here are the actual protocols and the networking subsystems of the relevant operating systems of your web servers and your networking equipment, such as switches and routers. Being able to telnet into a web server is essential, but this is only the first step. We need to understand the building blocks of the whole stack, how the model of operations and the operating systems start from low-level frames, move to a couple of layers of packets, then organize connections that are both fault-tolerant to an extent and may adapt to different characteristics of the underlying medium. The TCP/IP stack does not stand still. You will have to learn IPv6 deeply to be relevant in the coming years, for example. The application-level HTTP may seem simple at first glance, but you will also need to know everything about TLS. Debugging networking in your particular operating system is a whole separate discipline in itself. Although good knowledge of the *tcpdump* filter language is a very good start, it is usually not enough. Good little examples are the Nginx directives `tcp_nopush` and `tcp_nodelay`. Being able to explain what effect they have on the connections and predicting the change in user experience is what you want.

Specific backend software used in your company

Nginx is never the only software that powers your websites unless you only host a lot of static files. The upstream software is more often than not the source of problems with your site. Getting a good grasp of how a Ruby-on-Rails or Django application operates is not that hard, but being able to successfully deploy, monitor, and debug problems with a huge Java-based backend may be a whole new full-time job.

Modern cloud platforms

One of the few contexts where the buzzword "cloud" actually has a meaning, is the cloud hosting platforms field pioneered as a mass product by Amazon with its **Amazon Web Services (AWS)** but now represented by many players. Using one of those platforms is a recommended way of hosting a website unless you have very specific requirements. And mastering the platform is essential. Simpler solutions like the wildly popular Digital Ocean droplets are rather easy and do not diverge much from managing a real hardware server. AWS, on the contrary, is a huge ecosystem of interconnected complex products, such as databases, queueing/messaging services, and other specialized APIs that your developers will love to use. Having knowledge and practical experience with different platforms will be a great asset for you. By the way, `https://www.nginx.com` provides prebuilt AMIs with Nginx Plus, the commercial version of Nginx, for Amazon EC2 at `https://www.nginx.com/resources/admin-guide/setting-nginx-plus-environment-amazon-ec2/`.

Automation

There are two ways to scale manual labor: delegation to other people and automation. Although the first option is certainly important, the second is much preferred on the basis of cost. Knowing your *shell-fu* is again essential, but do have at least one general-purpose scripting language in your toolkit. The current fashion is Python or Ruby, whereas Node.js-based Javascript is emerging as another interesting choice. Perl is still very strong with its enormous library of open source, mostly bad but sometimes very good packages named CPAN. Recent Nginx versions have the ability to encapsulate scripting language interpreters into the web server. There was an official NginxScript JavaScript interpreter announced during the `nginx.conf` 2015 conference, and there is also a very popular module that embeds Lua. Refer to `https://openresty.org/`.

Proper automation skills will open new horizons for you, especially on the modern platforms that have APIs for traditionally manual tasks such as launching a new server. Automation is the key to scaling beyond a couple of servers to tens, hundreds, and more. This is where the DevOps engineering truly shines. Being able to create and launch a server farm into production from a script feels like a whole new dimension. When speaking about actual programming, there is the second path you may choose.

Software development

Nginx is developed by a commercial company having very highly qualified full-time paid software engineers. At the same time, the open source version of Nginx, which covers 99% of your needs, is always available both as a collection of versioned tarballs and as a Mercurial repository with commits history under a very permissive BSD license that allows modification and redistribution. This is a unique opportunity to learn from a corpus of very effective and professional C code. Nginx supports modules, and there are numerous third-party Nginx modules available (see the official wiki page `https://www.nginx.com/resources/wiki/modules/`). Nginx module development is the main way to customize the software for specific needs and is a very valuable skill that you may build your career on.

Nginx is written in C language with very little external dependencies. It contains its own highly effective library of primitive data structures and algorithms, such as hash tables, radix trees, and very efficient self-balancing red-black trees. Reading some clean-and-lean code is a special pleasure, and Nginx fully delivers on that front.

There are success stories about using customized Nginx as a web application platform, and for a great example, see the earlier-mentioned OpenResty. Although we cannot recommend this approach to businesses yet, being a developer in a company that has chosen Nginx as a platform may be a great way to become a rare specialist, who are always in high demand.

The most important benefit that you get from the open nature of Nginx combined with software engineering skills is an ultimate troubleshooting method: source-level debugging from inside Nginx. Nginx has great logging facilities, but nothing compares to the ability to step through critical sections in a debugger or modify the source to trigger rare conditions. And this brings us back to the main topic of this book. No matter how stable and robust Nginx has become over the years, it is still a piece of software that is written by humans and that is run in faulty, unpredictable, and mind-bogglingly complex environments. We hope that this book provided you with some new tools in your noble quest to run the fastest and the most valuable websites you can imagine.

Summary

In this final short chapter, we elaborated on different ways the readers may choose when they feel like moving forward as professionals with Nginx troubleshooting as one of their skills. The industry is so dynamic that you have to run just to stay in the same place, and this means learning and trying harder and harder with every coming day. We hope that our readers will make the modern web a better, more stable, and safe place with all the power that Nginx provides and will provide in future versions.

This (some will say "hopeless") desire for faster, more dependable websites and online services was the main motivation for the author of this book. The writing process had its easy and rough patches, but in the end, this dream is what always powered him. And the book was blessed with wonderful content managers.

Rare Nginx Error Messages

We conclude our book with a reference of interesting and not very common error messages that you might encounter in your log files. The table in this appendix may be an emergency reference or another peek into what could go wrong in your setup. In general, Nginx is pretty good at reporting its own problems. The messages usually have a standard format with common items, such as severity, function name, and pointers to external data that caused the problem.

We would recommend against leaving this table unread until a problem occurs because the notes column may contain interesting insights into how Nginx works and help you understand it better. Some of these messages you might not see in your real working experience, which is okay, as the error conditions are exceptions by definition.

could not open error log file: open() "/var/log/ nginx/error.log" failed	This is a very common error, which usually indicates problems with permissions on either the actual log files or the directory structure. You will see this in the `stderr` of the Nginx process because, obviously, it is an error in the error reporting mechanism.
rewrite or internal redirection cycle while internally redirecting	This message means you have a cycle in the rewrite/redirection logic. They may be introduced by complex regular expressions that match too much, for example.
invalid PID number $pid in $file	The saved PID number is garbled. There is a problem with the file that is mentioned in the `pid` directive of your `nginx.conf file`.
getpwnam($user) failed **getgrnam($group) failed**	These two mean that there are problems with the user and group that your Nginx is supposed to run as. This may happen when you try to use configuration files imported from other machines without corrections. See the documentation for the directive at `http://nginx.org/en/docs/ngx_core_module. html#user`.

could not build $hash, you should increase $hash_max_size: and **could not build $hash, you should increase $hash_bucket_size:**	These are the messages that Nginx emits when a hash table hits one of two limits — the total hash size and the size of each individual bucket. There are a number of hash tables used throughout the Nginx code, and all of them have the correspondent pairs of directives that look like `*_max_size` and `*_bucket_size`. You have to increase one of those values to get rid of the errors. Also, see the special document about hashes in Nginx at `http://nginx.org/en/docs/hash.html`.
read()/pread() read only $count of $size from $source	This message means that, unexpectedly, a reading syscall returned less bytes than it should have. There are a number of places where this kind of error may originate.
the configured event method cannot be used with thread pools	Thread pools require the epoll, eventport or the kqueue event subsystem.
pthread_create() failed	This and a number of similar errors come from the thread pool code that uses POSIX threads.
pcre_compile() failed:	Nginx uses the **Perl Compatible Regular Expressions (PCRE)** library to implement regexps. PCRE is fine and `pcre_compile()` is the function to compile a regular expression before matching it. Its failure indicates a bad regular expression.
pcre_study() failed: and **JIT compiler does not support pattern:**	Besides simple compilation, PCRE implements several heuristics to optimize the matching of some patterns. That is what `pcre_study()` does. There are very few ways for it to fail, but the JIT compiler, which is one of the optimizations, is a complex piece of software doing much work. Failure inside it probably means either a bug in PCRE or a very weird regular expression.
could not change the accept filter to $value	Accept filters are a feature of BSD kernels that allow postponing the return from the blocking `accept()` calls until there's a meaningful and expected piece of incoming data ready in the buffer. This is an internal error most probably indicating a bug.
$number worker_connections are not enough	You need to increase the number in the directive `worker_connections`.
rename() $filename1 to $filename2 failed before executing new binary process	During the very elaborate process of a graceful executable upgrade, Nginx tried to rename the `pid` file and failed. You may read about how Nginx manages to restart itself without losing connections at `http://nginx.org/en/docs/control.html`. See the USR2 signal.

the number of "worker_ processes" is not equal to the number of "worker_cpu_affinity" masks, using last mask for remaining worker processes	CPU affinity is a concept of tying worker processes to particular CPUs. The idea is to be able to say, for example, that the first worker should only run on the first four cores and the second worker should run on the second four cores, respectively.
	The number of affinity masks that you specify should correspond to the number of worker processes. If it is less, you get this warning message.
no "events" section in configuration	Your configuration file misses one of the most important sections, which is *Events*. See *Chapter 1, Searching for Problems in Nginx Configuration*.
$number worker_ connections exceed open file resource limit: $number	The resource limit on the number of open files (file descriptors limit) does not allow having as many worker connections as you wanted by specifying it with the worker_connections directive.
	See the ulimit manpage and also login.conf manpage if you are on FreeBSD.
"ssl_stapling" ignored, issuer certificate not found	A number of different messages all mentioning either SSL stapling (and the ssl_stapling directive) or OCSP may indicate that your HTTPS works not as efficiently as it could.
"ssl_stapling" ignored, no OCSP responder URL in the certificate	One of the most complex parts of all X.509 PKI is the issue of certificate revocation. OCSP is the newer attempt at providing online information about the revocation status of certificates, and in the worst case, it requires the client to regularly check the server certificate with an OCSP responder.
certificate status not found in the OCSP response	
OCSP responder timed out	When OCSP stapling is on, Nginx contacts the responder by itself and provides the clients with a signed, time-stamped OCSP ticket.
OCSP responder sent invalid "Content-Type" header:	Basically, a modern HTTPS website should have SSL stapling on and working. Fix these by following all the recommendations in the documentation closely.
nginx was built with Session Tickets support, however, now it is linked dynamically to an OpenSSL library which has no tlsext support, therefore Session Tickets are not available	**Server Name Indication (SNI)** is an HTTP request Host: header counterpart for HTTPS. It is a newer TLS/SSL feature, which permits name-based virtual hosting for HTTPS.
	The online Nginx documentation has a separate section on SNI at http://nginx.org/en/docs/http/configuring_ https_servers.html#sni.
and also the same about "SNI" instead of Session Tickets	Session Tickets is a TLS feature-optimizing handshake count.
	Both of these require OpenSSL support at compile time and at runtime.
	You may see these error messages when you run Nginx from a binary package on a box with bad OpenSSL.

open(/dev/poll) failed **kqueue() failed** **port_create() failed** **eventfd() failed**	These are all different indications that you have chosen the wrong event subsystem with the directive use in the events context. See `http://nginx.org/en/docs/events.html`.
no servers in upstream	Upstreams are groups of backends (whether they are separate hosts or just server software instances running locally) and you specified an empty group.
client intended to send too large body: $number bytes	Well-behaved HTTP clients indicate the size of the requests they send in the `Content-Length:` header. When this size exceeds the value from the `client_max_body_size` directive, Nginx will reject the request with a 413 code. The default value of this limit is only 1 MB, so you may face the problem very often if your website has a function of file uploads.
not well formed XML document	This very vague message is emitted from the rarely used XSLT module. It uses libxml2 and therefore needs valid XML documents.
FastCGI sent in stderr:	This is a message generated by the FastCGI upstream. FastCGI, as a protocol for communications with external processes, provides channels for both `stdout` and `stderr` of the backend software. So this is where `stderr` ends up.
no "proxy_ssl_ certificate_key" is defined **no proxy_ssl_trusted_ certificate for proxy_ ssl_verify**	Modern Nginx has the feature of being a good HTTPS client as well as a server. The HTTP proxy upstream is able to present a client certificate to an HTTPS upstream server. You will need to provide the key to the certificate as well. The client part also can verify the certificate of the server and even check it against a **Certificate Revocation List (CRL)**.
cache $zone uses the $path cache path while previously it used the $path cache path **cache $zone had previously different levels** **cache file $file is too small**	These messages indicate that the Nginx file cache directory was moved or otherwise tampered with. You should probably clean it and get ready to start again with a cold cache.
duplicate location $location	You have two exactly equal location selectors. Nginx will give you the line number of the second instance, but you will have to find the first yourself.

Index

A

alerts
  configuring 128, 129
Apache Flume 41
Apache migration problems
  defining 110, 111
  references 112
asynchronous inclusion 60

B

buffered access logging
  URL 25

C

Cacti
  URL 125
Certificate Revokation List (CRL) 148
CGI 80
Collectd
  URL 125
common mistakes, in Nginx configuration
  about 17
  file permissions 18
  regular expressions 19-21
  semicolons and newlines 17, 18
  variables 19
complain, processing
  about 50
  case journal, maintaining 52
  general HTTP response traffic, testing 54
  Internet connection test, performing 53
  Nginx configuration, keeping under
      source control 52
  rolling back 51
  simplest test, performing 53
conditional logging
  reference 35
Cyrillic charsets/encodings
  references 6

D

DDoS (Distributed Denial of Service) 57
debug logging
  URL 24
Denial of Service (DoS) 128
directive
  defining 87-89
Domain Validation (DV) 97

E

error_log directive documentation
  URL 43
etckeeper
  URL 52
external redirects
  replacing, with internal ones 93, 94

F

FastCGI responses
  URL, for caching 90
file upload progress bar
  displaying 113, 114
Fluentd 41
FS-Cache
  URL 92

functionality
troubleshooting 49, 50

G

general HTTP response traffic
integration failure 56
lying application, detecting 55, 56
monitoring, planning for 60
testing 54

H

HTTP auth
URL 27
HTTP status
URL 93
HTTP status code
URL 29
http_stub_status
parameters 121
statistics, obtaining from 120-125

I

idle upstream problem
references 116
solving 115
image filter module
URL 107
individual upstreams
Java backends 77, 78
optimizing 75
Perl backends, optimizing 79, 80
PHP backends, optimizing 76, 77
Python and Ruby backends,
optimizing 78, 79
static files, optimizing 76
integration failure
automatic removal from upstream,
setting up 58, 59
Server-Side Includes (SSI), configuring 60
try_files directive 57, 58
working around 56, 57

K

kibana 41

L

large_client_header_buffers directive
URL 47
log_format directive
URL 30
logs
about 23
creating 37
error log record 42-47
log data, defining 40, 41
log rotation, configuring 37-40
reading 41
logstash 41
Luameter
about 136
URL 136

M

mixed content warning, security warnings
references 104, 105
secure proxy, building
for external content 106, 107
URL 103
**Multipurpose Internet Mail Extensions
(MIME) 4**
Munin
about 125
Nginx, monitoring with 125-127
references 126

N

Nagios
URL 125
Nginx
about 1, 23, 141, 143
caching headers, emitting 82-86
caching layer 82
defining 72-75
monitoring, with Munin 1250127
Nginx upstream modules, caching 87-91
references 48, 142
restarting 67
restart modes 67, 68
static files, caching 91, 92

status, obtaining from 130-135
thread pools, using 81
Nginx blog post
  URL 81
Nginx configuration
  about 2
  basic configuration syntax 2
  common mistakes 17
  default configuration directory layout 5, 6
  default nginx.conf 9
  directives 2
  http directive 10-16
  include directive 4
  MIME types registry, modifying 7, 8
  multiline directives 3, 4
  simple directives 3
  testing 5
Nginx documentation
  reference 12
  URL 87
Nginx error messages
  defining 145-148
  references 145
Nginx expires directive
  values, defining 85
Nginx logging
  big request bodies, logging 36
  conditional logging 35
  configuring 23-26, 30-32
  POST requests, logging 32-35
  references 34
Nginx-lua-stats
  about 136
  URL 136
Nginx modules
  references 107
  URL 143
Nginx-module-vts
  URL 136
Nginx plugins
  URL 126
Nginx Plus
  URL 130
Nginx Plus alternatives
  Luameter 136
  Nginx-lua-stats 136

Nginx-module-vts 136
requests/sec patch, by Catap 138
upsteam_check module 137
using 135
Ustats module 138
Nginx Plus web page
  URL 130
nginx_status
  URL 126
ngxtop
  URL 118
  using 118, 119
no traffic situation
  processing 61-66

O

obsolete pages
  and VirtualBox 110
OpenNMS
  URL 125
OpenResty
  URL 142

P

patch
  URL 138
PCRE documentation
  reference 15
Perl 80
**Perl Compatible Regular Expressions
  (PCRE) 146**
Perl Server Gateway Interface 80
problem solving
  with cache 108, 109
  with WebSockets 112
PSGI 80

R

request bodies
  reference 36
RFC1413
  URL 27
Ruby
  URL 79

S

SANs (Subject Alternative Name) 99
Scribe 41
secure link module
  URL 107
security warnings
  about 96
  Domain name mismatch 97-99
  expired certificates 100, 101
  insecure warnings, for valid certificates 101
  mixed content warning 102-105
  references 96
Server Name Indication (SNI) 147
Server-Side Includes (SSI) 60
SlowFS
  about 92
  URL 92
Snitch
  URL 101
software development
  defining 143
Splunk 41
statistics
  obtaining, from http_stub_status 120-125
status, Nginx Plus
  URL 130
status_zone directive
  URL 135
system administration
  automation 142
  backend software, using 141
  defining 140
  Linux 140
  modern cloud platforms 142
  modern Internet protocols 141
  Unix 140

T

tarball
  reference 2
thread pools
  used, in Nginx 81
traffic
  investigating 69

U

upsteam_check module
  about 137
  URL 137
User-generated Content (UGC) 105
Ustats module
  URL 138

V

variables, Nginx
  URL 30
VirtualBox
  and obsolete pages 110

W

Web Server Gateway Interface (WSGI) 78
WebSockets 112
World Wide Web (WWW) 6

Y

Yahoo
  URL 93

Z

Zabbix
  URL 125

www.ingramcontent.com/pod-product-compliance
Lightning Source LLC
Chambersburg PA
CBHW060137060326
40690CB00018B/3916